Wasmuth & Zohlen Verlag

Franco Stella

Berliner Schloss – Humboldt Forum

Konstruktion	Costruzione	Construction
und Rekonstruktion	e ricostruzione	and Reconstruction
der Architektur	dell'architettura	of the Architecture

Vorwort   Prefazione   Preface   **Horst Bredekamp**

Wasmuth & Zohlen Verlag

Vorwort	Prefazione	Preface

Horst Bredekamp
Coincidentia Oppositorum

Geschichte und Gegenwart sind kommunizierende Röhren: So, wie sich die Gegenwart als ein spannungsreiches Produkt der Historie erweist, so wird das Bild der Geschichte von Prozessen mitgeprägt, die sich aus der Reflexion der jeweiligen Jetztzeit ergeben. Ein Paradebeispiel dafür ist das Gebäude des Humboldt Forums: Mit ihm wird eine entschiedene Reformulierung der Geschichte Berlins vollzogen. Mit seinem Bau zeigt Franco Stella, dass er über ein tiefes Verständnis für die Geschichtlichkeit des Berliner Schlosses und dessen architektonische Einbettung verfügt. Sein Bauwerk ist keinesfalls nur ein Palast oder ein Schloss, sondern ein Stadtteil, dessen Portale nicht nur als eine zu durchschreitende Grenze, sondern vielmehr als eine sich zu beiden Seiten in Plätze öffnende Architektur konzipiert wurden und damit die einstmals vorhandene Urbanität in die Mitte Berlins zurückzuholen sucht.

Dasselbe gilt noch mehr für die Passage und die Blickachse, die sich

La storia e il presente sono vasi comunicanti: se il presente è il prodotto ricco di tensioni della storia, l'immagine della storia è plasmata da processi risultanti dalla riflessione ad essi contemporanea. Un esempio paradigmatico di ciò è l'edificio dell'Humboldt Forum: con esso si compie una riformulazione decisiva della storia di Berlino. Con la sua costruzione, Franco Stella mostra di avere una profonda comprensione della storicità del Castello di Berlino e del suo inserimento architettonico. Il suo edificio non è un semplice palazzo o un castello, ma una parte di città, i cui portali non sono stati pensati solo come un confine da attraversare, ma soprattutto come un'architettura che si apre in piazze su entrambi i lati, cercando così di riportare nel centro di Berlino l'urbanità che esisteva un tempo.

Lo stesso vale ancora di più per il cosiddetto Passage e per l'asse visivo che, a partire da sud, attraversa il cortile Schlüterhof e arriva alla facciata dell'Alte Nationalgalerie. Gli atrii dei portali hanno una fun-

History and the present are communicating vessels: if the present is the tension-rich product of history, the image of history is shaped by processes resulting from contemporary reflection. A paradigmatic example of this is the building of the Humboldt Forum: with it, a decisive reformulation of Berlin's history takes place. With its construction, Franco Stella shows that he has a profound understanding of the historicity of the Berlin Palace and its architectural insertion. His building is not merely a palace or a castle, but a part of city, the portals of which were conceived not only as a border to be crossed, but above all as an architecture that opens up into squares on both sides, attempting to bring back the urbanity that once existed in the centre of Berlin.

The same applies even more to the so-called Passage and the visual axis that, starting from the south, crosses the Schlüterhof courtyard and arrives at the façade of the Alte Nationalgalerie. The atriums of the portals have a transitional function

durch den Schlüterhof von Süden her bis zur Fassade der Alten Nationalgalerie ergibt. Die Durchgänge haben eine transitorische Funktion, die sie bis zum Ende der Blickmöglichkeit über ihre eigentliche Funktion hinaustreiben. Architektur ist für Stella eine Ermöglichungsform, die mit dem Menschen, ihren Blicken und Bewegungen in Verbindung steht. Sie stellt das Gegenteil von jenem Gestus dar, der ihm gelegentlich mit Furor entgegengehalten worden ist: dem einer kalten Rationalität.

Stella denkt in Spannungen. Sein 2007 im Stile eines Manifestes in »AIÓN« veröffentlichter Text *L'Architettura e la Costruzione* zielt auf die aus der Geschichte abgeleitete Begründung einer Architektur ab, die als *Coincidentia oppositorum*, als Zusammenfall von Gegenpolen, zu begreifen ist. Stella erweist sich in diesem Text als ein Strukturalist, der eine Versöhnung zwischen zwei Prinzipien intendiert: einerseits der Funktion des Tragens, also der Wand, und andererseits der Symbo-

zione transitoria che, oltre a quella del passaggio, si estende fino alla fine della possibilità di visione. Per Stella, l'architettura è un mondo di possibilità che si offre alle persone, ai loro sguardi e movimenti: giusto l'opposto di quel gesto furioso che talvolta gli è stato lanciato contro, accusandolo di fredda razionalità.

Il pensiero di Stella è teso fra elementi opposti. Il suo testo *L'Architettura e la Costruzione*, pubblicato su «AIÓN» nel 2007 nello stile di un manifesto, mira alla fondazione, giustificata dalla Storia, di un'architettura come *coincidentia oppositorum*, come coincidenza di poli opposti. In questo testo, Stella dimostra d'essere uno strutturalista che intende conciliare due principi: quello della funzione portante, rappresentato dal muro, e quello della simbolizzazione di sé stessa, con il motivo architettonico particolarmente eloquente del trilite. Come mostra uno dei modelli originali della struttura di Stonehenge (fig. 1), si tratta di due elementi portanti verticali, sopra i quali è disposto orizzontalmente l'e-

which, in addition to that of passage, extends to the end of the possibility of vision. For Stella, architecture is a world of possibilities that offers itself to people, their gazes and movements: just the opposite of the furious gesture that has sometimes been thrown at him, accusing him of cold rationality.

Stella's thinking is stretched between opposite elements. His text *L'Architettura e la Costruzione*, published on "AIÓN" in 2007, in the style of a manifesto, aims at the foundation, justified by History, of architecture as *coincidentia oppositorum*, as the coincidence of opposite poles. In this text, Stella shows himself to be a structuralist who intends to reconcile two principles: on the one hand that of the load-bearing function, represented by the wall, and on the other that of the symbolisation of itself with the particularly eloquent architectural motif of the Trilite. As shown in one of the original models in the form of the Stonehenge structure (fig. 1), it consists of two vertical supporting elements,

Abb. 1: Der Trilith von Stonehenge
Fig. 1: Il Trilite di Stonehenge
Fig. 1: The Trilite of Stonehenge

Abb. 2: Das Erechtheion auf der Akropolis von Athen
Fig. 2: L'Erechtheion dell'Acropoli di Atene
Fig. 2: The Erechtheion of the Acropolis in Athens

lisierung ihrer selbst in einem besonders sprechenden Architekturmotiv, dem Trilith. Wie es eines der Urmodelle in Form der Gebilde von Stonehenge zeigt (Abb. 1), handelt es sich um eine Doppelstütze, über die ein Querbalken gelegt ist. Als autonomes Gebilde kann der Trilith von der tragenden Wand gelöst werden, sodass dieses Architekturelement zunächst nichts als sich selbst trägt.

Es bietet damit die Möglichkeit, die tragenden Stützen in unterschiedlichen Formen aufzuführen, so vor allem als Pfeiler oder als Säule, die eine Verbindung zur menschlichen Gestalt als sich selbst tragender, aufrechter Größe anzeigen. Hierin, wie etwa im Erechtheion auf der Akropolis (Abb. 2), liegt, um ein großes Wort zu nutzen, die Humanität einer Architektur, welche nicht allein die Funktion der Stütze, sondern auch deren autonomes Dekorum als Symbolisierung ihrer selbst aufnimmt. Die gesamte Architekturgeschichte ist Stella zufolge davon bestimmt, dieses den menschlichen Proportionen zugängliche Element mit der rei-

lemento portato. Come costruzione autonoma, il trilite può essere staccato dal muro di sostegno, e almeno inizialmente non sostenere altro che sé stesso.

Aprendo così la possibilità di realizzare gli elementi portanti in forme diverse, inanzitutto o come pilastri o come colonne, che possono prendere a modello la figura umana, eretta e autoportante. Nel caso in esame, quasi come nell'Erechtheion dell'Acropoli (fig. 2), risiede, per usare una grande parola, l'umanità di un'architettura che non solo assume la funzione del sostegno, ma anche quella del suo decoro autonomo come simbolizzazione di sé stessa. Secondo Stella, l'intera storia dell'architettura è caratterizzata dalla combinazione dell'ordine delle colonne, con proporzioni a scala umana, con l'ordine della costruzione, rappresentato dai muri portanti.

L'architetto Andrea Palladio, da Stella particolarmente ammirato, interpreta questo principio quando, a metà del XVI secolo, erige i suoi co-

above which the bearing element is arranged horizontally. As an autonomous construction, the trilithon can be detached from the supporting wall, and at least initially support nothing but itself.

This opens up the possibility of realising the bearing elements in different forms, first of all either as pillars or as columns, which can take the human figure, upright and self-supporting, as a model. In this case, almost as in the Erechtheion of the Acropolis (fig. 2), lies, to use a great word, the humanity of an architecture that not only assumes the function of support, but also that of its autonomous decoration as a symbolisation of itself. According to Stella, the entire history of architecture is characterised by the combination of the order of columns, with proportions on a human scale, with the order of the construction, represented by load-bearing walls.

The architect Andrea Palladio, whom Stella particularly admired, interpreted this principle when he erected his colonnades in the mid-

Abb. 3: Die Loggien der Basilica Palliadiana in Vicenza
Fig. 3: Le Logge della Basilica Palladiana a Vicenza
Fig. 3: The Loggias of the Basilica Palladiana in Vicenza

Abb. 4: Der Palazzo dei Conservatori von Michelangelo in Rom
Fig. 4: Il Palazzo dei Conservatori a Roma di Michelangelo
Fig. 4: The Michelangelo's Palazzo dei Conservatori in Rome

nen Funktion einer tragenden Wand zu verbinden.

Der von Stella in besonderer Weise verehrte Architekt Andrea Palladio hat dieses Prinzip in Form einer Durchsäulung der Wandöffnungen in der Mitte des 16. Jahrhunderts bei allen Stockwerken des Palazzo della Ragione von Vicenza angewendet (Abb. 3). Es muss für Stella ein Faszinosum gewesen sein, zu erkennen, wie Andreas Schlüter in seiner Architektur des Berliner Schlosses mit dieser Zusammenführung von Wand und Proportionssymbol umgegangen ist. Bis heute beeindruckt, wie Schlüter, auf den Konservatorenpalast Michelangelos auf dem Kapitol von Rom anspielend (Abb. 4), im unteren Stock des Berliner Ostflügels die Säulen auf eine in funktionaler Sicht widersinnige Weise in die Wand eingestellt hat (Abb. 5). Schlüter hat zudem kolossale Säulen vor den Mitteltrakt des nach ihm benannten Hofes gesetzt, um ihnen keine weitere Funktion zuzubilligen als allein diejenige, den Reigen von überlebensgroßen Skulp-

lonnati davanti alle pareti finestrate del Palazzo della Ragione di Vicenza (fig. 3). Deve essere stato affascinante per Stella sapere come Andreas Schlüter, nella sua architettura del Castello di Berlino, abbia risolto la combinazione del muro con il simbolo dell'umana proporzione. Ancora oggi è impressionante come Schlüter, in analogia al Palazzo dei Conservatori di Michelangelo nel Campidoglio a Roma (fig. 4), abbia inserito le colonne nel muro del piano inferiore dell'ala est del Castello di Berlino, senza alcuna giustificazione funzionale (fig. 5). Schlüter ha anche collocato colonne colossali davanti al tratto centrale della facciata est della corte che porta il suo nome: colonne che non hanno altra funzione se non quella di sostenere i piedistalli su cui poggiano le statue a grandezza d'uomo (fig. 6). Qui si gioca con l'architettura per trasformarla in una parabola scultorea di sé stessa.

Un altro significativo elemento di questo edificio è la non-romantica cucitura tra l'architettura di Schlüter

16th century in front of the windowed walls of the Palazzo della Ragione in Vicenza (fig. 3). It must have been fascinating for Stella to learn how Andreas Schlüter, in his Berlin Palace architecture, solved the combination of the wall with the symbol of human proportion. Till today it is impressive how Schlüter, in analogy to Michelangelo's Palazzo dei Conservatori on the Capitol in Rom (fig. 4), inserted the columns into the wall on the lower floor of the east wing of Berlin Palace without any functional justification (fig. 5). Schlüter also placed colossal columns in front of the central section of the east façade of the courtyard that is named after him: columns that have no function other than to support the pedestals on which the life-size statues rest (fig. 6). Here, architecture is played with to turn it into a sculptural parable of itself.

Another significant element of this building is the non-romantic seam between Schlüter's and Stella's architecture. The crucial point is the transition from east wing to Schlüter's

Abb. 5: Das rekonstruierte Portal des Schlüterhofs

Fig. 5: Il ricostruito Portale della corte Schlüterhof

Fig. 5: The reconstructed Portal of the courtyard Schlüterhof

Schlüterhof
Abb. 6: Blick auf die rekonstruierten Ost- und Nordfassaden

Fig. 6: Veduta delle ricostruite facciate est e nord

Fig. 6: View of the reconstructed east and north façades

turen zu tragen (Abb. 6). Hier wird mit der Architektur gespielt, um diese zum skulpturalen Gleichnis ihrer selbst zu machen.

Ein weiteres Element der Architektur liegt in der unromantischen Naht zwischen Schlüters und Stellas Trakten. Das entscheidende Moment ist der Übergang von Stellas Ostflügel zu den rekonstruierten Flügeln Schlüters im Norden und Süden. Stella hat den Übergang nicht verschliffen; vielmehr in genau jenem Grat, an dem beide Stilformen aneinanderstoßen, eine Fuge gesetzt, die bei dem sich wandelnden Licht wechselnd dunkler oder heller aufscheint, um als sprechende Architektur zu betonen: »Wir sind autonom« (Abb. 7).

In der zum Eosanderhof hinüberführenden Passage sind die Ost- und Westfassaden durch Stellas Stil bestimmt, sodass sich hier nun anders als im Schlüterhof die aktuellen Seiten in gleicher Gliederung gegenüberstehen. In diesem Trakt hat Stella die Verbindung von Gegensätzen dadurch ausgespielt, dass er im

e quella di Stella. Il punto cruciale è il passaggio dalla sua ala est alle ricostruite ali nord e sud di Schlüter. Stella non ha addolcito la transizione; anzi, proprio la linea d'intersezione dei due linguaggi è una fuga che appare alternativamente più scura o più chiara al variare della luce, quasi a dichiarare l'uno e l'altro la propria autonomia (fig. 7).

Nel Passage ricavato nell'Eosanderhof, le facciate est e ovest sono definite dallo stile di Stella, cosicché qui, a differenza dello Schlüterhof, le facciate che oggi si fronteggiano presentano la stessa articolazione architettonica. In questo luogo Stella ha messo in scena la combinazione degli opposti erigendo davanti alle facciate dei lati maggiori, in analogia alle colonne d'ordine gigante di Schlüter, un'intera foresta di colonne, che dimostrano il principio del trilite come forma simbolica (fig. 8). Non si tratta di arbitrio, ma del rifiuto consapevole di una razionalità puramente funzionale, che non riconosce l'importanza dell'analogia antropomor-

reconstructed north and south wings. Stella has not softened the transition; on the contrary, the very line of intersection of the two languages is a fugue that appears alternately darker or lighter as the light changes, almost as if to declare one and the other its autonomy (fig. 7).

In the Passage in the Eosanderhof, the east and west façades are defined by Stella's style, so that here, in contrast to the Schlüterhof, the façades facing each other today present the same architectural articulation. Here, Stella has staged the combination of opposites by erecting a whole forest of columns in front of the façades on the longer sides, in analogy to Schlüter's giant order columns, demonstrating the trilithon principle as a symbolic form (fig. 8). This is not arbitrariness, but the conscious rejection of a purely functional rationality, which fails to recognise the importance of anthropological analogy for the reception of architectural forms.

Finally, in the former Eosanderhof court, the trilithic symbolic func-

Abb. 7: Blick auf das rekonstruierte Eckturm-Rondell

Fig. 7: Veduta della ricostruita torretta d'angolo-Rondell

Fig. 7: View of the reconstructed corner turret-Rondell

Passage
Abb. 8: Blick auf die neue via colonnata und das rekonstruierte Portal IV. Im Hintergrund: die Kolonnade des Alten Museums

Fig. 8: Vista della nuova via colonnata e del ricostruito portale IV. Sul fondo: il colonnato dell'Altes Museum

Fig. 8: View of the new via colonnata and the reconstructed Portal IV. In the background: the colonnade of the Altes Museum

Sinne von Schlüters Kolossalsäulen an die langen Seitenwände einen ganzen Wald von Säulen stellte, der das Prinzip des Triliths in symbolischer Form aufführt (Abb. 8). Hierin liegt keine Willkür, sondern die bewusste Zurückweisung rein funktionaler Rationalität, die ohne Beziehung zur körperschematischen Rezeption des Menschen bleibt.

Im Eosanderhof schließlich wird die zum Bogen veränderte trilithische Symbolfunktion der Architektur zum Theater ihrer selbst (Abb. 9). Hier ist im Unterschied zum Schlüterhof das Verhältnis zwischen Geschichte und Moderne umgekehrt: Den drei von Stella geprägten Seitenwänden und Galerien steht die Rekonstruktion des Eosanderportals gegenüber, das seinerseits mit dem riesigen Triumphbogen an den Konstantins- und den Septimius-Severus-Bogen vom Forum Romanum in Rom appelliert und wie eine Theaterszene an die Bühne gestellt ist.

Mauern und Trilithen, Stützfunktion und humanisierendes Dekor, Portal und Platzöffnung, Blick-

fica per la ricezione delle forme dell'architettura.

Infine, nell'ex corte Eosanderhof, la funzione simbolica trilitica dell'architettura, trasformata in arco, diventa teatro di sé stessa (fig. 9). Qui, rispetto allo Schlüterhof, il rapporto tra storia e modernità è capovolto: alle tre pareti laterali con le gallerie modellate da Stella si aggiunge il ricostruito Portale di Eosander, il cui enorme arco di trionfo ricorda l'Arco di Costantino e l'Arco di Settimio Severo del Foro Romano, e qui funge da fronte di scena di un'aula-teatro.

Muri e triliti, funzione portante e decoro a misura umana, portali e apertura dei luoghi, indirizzo e ampliamento della vista, fissazione dell'elemento costruttivo e trasformazione nel suo opposto: sono questi i principi che Franco Stella ha sviluppato in modo ostinato e originale nella cerchia dei suoi colleghi di Venezia, fra i quali Aldo Rossi e Manfredo Tafuri. Con l'Humboldt Forum, ritorna un alito mediterraneo. Dopo che Andreas Schlüter aveva

tion of architecture, transformed into an arch, becomes a theatre of itself (fig. 9). Here, in comparison to the Schlüterhof, the relationship between history and modernity is reversed: the three side walls with the galleries modelled by Stella are joined by the reconstructed Eosander portal, whose enormous triumphal arch is reminiscent of the Arch of Constantine and the Arch of Septimius Severus in the Roman Forum, and here serves as the front of a theatre scene.

Walls and Trilites, load-bearing function and decoration to human measure, portals and the opening up of places, addressing and widening the view, fixing the building elements and transforming it into its opposite: these are the principles that Franco Stella developed in an original and obstinate way in the circle of his colleagues in Venice, including Aldo Rossi and Manfredo Tafuri. With the Humboldt Forum, a Mediterranean breath returns. After Andreas Schlüter had offered the Prussian king a building that represented

Abb. 9: Blick auf das rekonstruierte Portal III und die neuen Loggien

Fig. 9: Veduta del ricostruito Portale III e dei nuovi loggiati

Fig. 9: View of the reconstructed Portal III and the new loggias

lenkung und Blickerweiterung, Fixierung des Bauelementes und Überführung in sein Gegenteil: dies sind jene Prinzipien, die Franco Stella auf eigenwillige Weise im Umkreis seiner Kollegen in Venedig mit Aldo Rossi und Manfredo Tafuri gemeinsam entwickelt hat. Durch das Humboldt Forum wird ein mittelmeerisches Anliegen erneut präsent. Nachdem Andreas Schlüter dem preußischen König ein Gebäude geboten hatte, das bis in die Details eine Übertragung von römischen Formen nach Brandenburg darstellte, stellt Franco Stellas Humboldt Forum wiederum ein Element jener *Italianità* dar, die das Stadtgefüge Berlins in zahlreichen Fassungen verwandelt hat: nicht nur seiner Form, sondern auch seinem gedanklichen Anspruch nach stellt er Berlin ans Mittelmeer (vgl. H. Bredekamp, *Berlin am Mittelmeer*, 2018). Indem das Schloss zu einem Gefüge italienischer Piazze wurde, ist es nicht nur eine Blick-, Bewegungs- und Formschule, sondern auch eine Übung im Denken. Darin transzendiert es un-

offerto al re prussiano un edificio che rappresentava, fin nei dettagli, il trasferimento di forme romane nel Brandeburgo, fin nei dettagli, l'Humboldt Forum di Franco Stella rappresenta a sua volta un elemento di quell'*italianità* che ha trasformato in tanti diversi modi il tessuto urbano berlinese: non solo per la sua forma, ma anche per le sue aspirazioni intellettuali, si può parlare di Berlino sul Mediterraneo (cfr. H. Bredekamp, *Berlin am Mittelmeer*, 2018). Diventato una compagine di piazze italiane, il Castello non è solo una scuola di visione, movimento e forma, ma anche un esercizio di pensiero. In questo modo trascende il nostro tempo presente, che sostituisce sempre più spesso con prospettive lineari la complessità dei processi che riescono a risolvere in armonia le contraddizioni.

Per quanto siano impressionanti gli elementi delle parti ricostruite e di nuova concezione dell'architettura dell'Humboldt Forum, è deplorevole il fatto che la sua costruzione, sebbene terminata, non sia del tutto

the transfer of Roman forms to Brandenburg, right down to the details, Franco Stella's Humboldt Forum in turn represents an element of that *italianity* that has transformed Berlin's urban fabric in so many different ways: not only because of its form, but also because of its intellectual aspirations, one can speak of Berlin on the Mediterranean (see H. Bredekamp, *Berlin am Mittelmeer*, 2018). Having become a compendium of Italian piazzas, the Berlin Palace is not only a school of vision, movement and form, but also an exercise in thought. In this way, it transcends our present time, which increasingly substitutes linear perspectives for the complexity of processes that manage to resolve contradictions in harmony.

As impressive as the elements of the reconstructed and newly conceived parts of the architecture of the Humboldt Forum are, it is regrettable that its construction, although completed, is not quite finished. Stella's architecture lives not only from the perforation of the walls in

sere Jetztzeit, die zunehmend lineare Perspektiven an die Stelle von komplexen, Widersprüche in Harmonie bringenden Verfahren setzt.

So eindrucksvoll sich die Elemente der rekonstruierten wie der neu konzipierten Teile der Architektur des Humboldt Forums ausnehmen, so bedauernswert ist es, dass ihre Erbauung, obwohl beendet, nicht vollendet werden konnte. Stellas Architektur lebt nicht allein von der Perforation von Wänden in jeweils zu zwei Seiten sich öffnende Plätze, sondern auch von der Resonanz von Begegnungen im Inneren. Sein Modell ist die Überführung der statischen Elemente in Requisiten des Theaters, wie sie im 17. Jahrhundert gebräuchlich war. Die Besonderheit dieses Prinzips liegt darin, dass die auf den Emporen präsenten Skulpturen mit den Besuchern von Kirchen oder Palästen auf eine Weise zusammenspielen, als würden lebendige Wesen miteinander kommunizieren. Das wohl berühmteste Beispiel stellt die Cornaro-Kapelle der römischen Kirche Santa Maria della

compiuta. L'architettura di Stella non vive solo della perforazione dei muri in rapporto alle due piazze su cui prospetta, ma anche della risonanza degli incontri al loro interno. Il suo ideale è la trasfigurazione degli elementi statici in elementi del teatro, come era comune nel XVII secolo. La particolarità di questo principio sta nel fatto che le sculture presenti nelle gallerie interagiscono con i visitatori delle chiese o dei palazzi come se fossero esseri viventi che comunicano con loro. Forse l'esempio più famoso in questo senso è la Cappella Cornaro della chiesa romana di Santa Maria della Vittoria, sulle cui gallerie figure di persone eccitate recitano l'adorazione eterna, mentre sull'altare maggiore la Santa Teresa di Gianlorenzo Bernini va in estasi (fig. 10).

Stella aveva auspicato la presenza di visitatori nelle gallerie del Foyer, quali sculture viventi di una rappresentazione teatrale, in comunicazione con i nuovi arrivati. Per spingere i visitatori a entrare nelle gallerie proponeva l'inserimento

relation to the two squares in which it faces, but also from the resonance of the encounters within them. His ideal is the transfiguration of static elements into elements of theatre, as was common in the 17th century. The peculiarity of this principle lies in the fact that the sculptures in the galleries interact with the visitors to the churches or palaces as if they were living beings communicating with them. Perhaps the most famous example in this respect is the Cornaro Chapel in the Roman church of Santa Maria della Vittoria, on whose galleries figures of excited persons staging the eternal adoration, while on the high altar St. Theresa by Gianlorenzo Bernini goes into ecstasy (fig. 10).

Stella had hoped for the presence of visitors in the galleries of the Foyer, as living sculptures of a theatrical performance, in communication with newcomers. To encourage visitors to enter the galleries, he proposed the insertion of showcases in the niches of the walls, in which to display objects *en miniature* from

Abb. 10: Die Familie Corner erlebt die Ekstase der Heiligen Theresa von Gianlorenzo Bernini in der Kirche von Santa Maria della Vittoria in Rom

Fig. 10: La famiglia Corner assiste all'estasi di santa Teresa di Gianlorenzo Bernini nella chiesa di Santa Maria della Vittoria a Roma

Fig. 10: The Corner family attends the Ecstasy of Saint Theresa by Gianlorenzo Bernini in the church of Santa Maria della Vittoria in Rome

Vittoria dar, in der erregte Personen auf den Emporen die ewige Anbetung darbieten, während auf dem Hochaltar die heilige Theresa von Gianlorenzo Bernini in Verzückung gerät (Abb. 10).

Stella hat mit Blick auf die Stockwerke des Foyers darauf gesetzt, dass sich die Besucher auf den Brüstungen wie in einem Theaterstück als gleichsam lebendige Skulpturen zeigen und mit den Neuankömmlingen in eine Kommunikation treten. Die zum Betreten der Emporen verlockenden Magneten sollten die in die Wände eingelassenen Vitrinen darstellen, in denen im Stil der frühneuzeitlichen Kunstkammern Gegenstände aus den Reichen der Natur, der Kunsttechnologie und der Kunst *en miniature* gezeigt werden sollten. Auf diese Weise wäre jene Uridee einer lebendigen und ›wilden‹ Kunstkammer als Leitmotiv entfaltet worden, wie sie im Berliner Schloss bis zu deren Auflösung im späten 19. Jahrhundert vorhanden war. So wäre die Idee des Sammelns aufgenommen worden, die vom *objet*

nelle nicchie delle pareti di vetrine, in cui esporre oggetti *en miniature* del regno della natura, della tecnologia e dell'arte, evocativi delle Kunstkammer del vecchio Castello. In questo modo, quell'idea originaria sarebbe stata il *leitmotiv* di una Kunstkammer viva e 'selvaggia' come lo era stata nel Castello di Berlino fino alla sua dissoluzione alla fine del XIX secolo. In questo modo sarebbe stata ripresa l'idea del collezionismo, che spaziava dall'*objet trouvé* delle avanguardie del XX secolo all'*arte povera* dei nostri giorni. È stato questo il concetto presentato da me nel 2001, accettato dalla Commissione «Historische Mitte Berlin» e poi confermato dal Bundestag. In questo modo, Stella sperava di riscattare il suo concetto di architettura del Foyer come *theatrum mundi*.

Questo non è stato realizzato e quindi l'immagine di una vivace comunicazione fra persone che guardano le vetrine delle gallerie e i visitatori nel Foyer è stata sostituita da quella metafisica di morte aper-

the realm of nature, technology and art, evocative of the Kunstkammer of the old Palace. In this way, that original idea would have been the *leitmotiv* of a living and 'wild' Kunstkammer as it had been in the Berlin Palace until its dissolution at the end of the 19th century. In this way, the idea of collecting, ranging from the *objet trouvé* of the 20th century avant-gardes to the *poor art* of today, would have been revived. This was the concept presented by myself in 2001, accepted by the "Historische Mitte Berlin" Commission and then confirmed by the Bundestag. In this way, Stella hoped to redeem his concept of the architecture of the Foyer as *theatrum mundi*.

This was not realised and so the image of lively communication between people looking at the gallery windows and visitors in the foyer was replaced by the metaphysical one of death aperture. But the Humboldt Forum has not come to an end; it is a process, and so it remains to be hoped and hoped that

trouvé der Avantgarde des 20. Jahrhunderts bis zur *arte povera* unserer Gegenwart reichte. Es war jenes Konzept, das von mir 2001 vorgestellt, von der Kommission »Historische Mitte Berlin« angenommen und vom Deutschen Bundestag bestätigt wurde. Stella hoffte, auf diese Weise sein Konzept der Architektur des Foyers als *Theatrum mundi* einzulösen.

Dies ist nicht realisiert worden, und daher ergibt sich im Foyer keine vitale Kommunikation zwischen den die Vitrinen betrachtenden Personen und den im Foyer befindlichen Besuchern, sondern ein eher metaphysisches Panorama toter Öffnungen. Aber das Humboldt Forum ist nicht am Ende; es ist ein Prozess, und damit bleibt zu wünschen und zu hoffen, dass Stellas Vision einer Architektur humaner Lebendigkeit auch als Binnentheater zukünftig eine Erfüllung erfährt.

ture. Ma l'Humboldt Forum non è arrivato alla fine; è un processo, e quindi resta da augurarsi e sperare che la visione di Stella di un'architettura di umana vitalitá trovi in futuro una realizzazione anche come teatro interno.

Stella's vision of an architecture of human vitality will also be realised as an indoor theatre in the future.

S. 16/17: Blick auf den neuen Spreeflügel und die rekonstruierte Südfassade

P. 16/17: Veduta del nuovo edificio sulla Sprea e della ricostruita facciata sud

P. 16/17: View of the new building towards the Spree and the reconstructed south façade

Einführung **Introduzione** **Introduction**

Am 4. Juli 2002 beschloss der Deutsche Bundestag auf Empfehlung der Internationalen Expertenkommission »Historische Mitte Berlin«, dass sich die »Bebauung des Berliner Schlossplatzes [...] an der Stereometrie des ehemaligen Berliner Schlosses orientieren« solle und für das neue Gebäude »die Wiedererrichtung der barocken Fassaden der Nord-, West- und Südseite sowie den Schlüterhof des ehemaligen Schlosses vorzusehen«[1] sei.

Dass ich in meinem Entwurf für den Wettbewerb »Wiederaufbau des Berliner Schlosses – Bau des Humboldt-Forums« 2008 diese Entscheidung des deutschen Parlaments respektierte, führte unvermeidlich zu Konflikten mit einigen tief verwurzelten ideologischen Grundsätzen der modernen / zeitgenössischen Baukultur. Insbesondere mit der Auffassung, dass ein rekonstruiertes Gebäude niemals authentisch sein könne, selbst wenn es an seinen ursprünglichen Standort zurückkehrt, sowie der Vorstellung, dass die Form einer

Il Parlamento tedesco, il 4 Luglio 2002, facendo propria la raccomandazione della Commissione internazionale degli Esperti «Historische Mitte Berlin», decise che «l'edificazione della Schlossplatz deve orientarsi alla stereometria del perduto Castello di Berlino» e «l'architettura del nuovo edificio deve prevedere la ricostruzione delle facciate barocche dei lati nord, ovest e sud, nonché dello Schlüterhof del Castello perduto».[1]

Rispettando tale decisione, il mio progetto per il Concorso «Ricostruzione del Castello di Berlino – Costruzione dello Humboldt Forum» del 2008, era destinato a confliggere con alcuni radicati fondamenti ideologici della moderna / contemporanea cultura architettonica. In particolare con l'idea che un edificio ricostruito non possa essere autentico, neanche quando ritorna nel luogo in cui si trovava, e con l'idea che l'antica forma di una facciata ricostruita sia incompatibile con una moderna configurazione e funzione degli spazi interni.

On 4 July 2002, the German Parliament, following the recommendation of the International Commission of Experts "Historische Mitte Berlin", decided "that the development of the Schlossplatz" should be modelled "on the stereometry of the former Berlin Palace" and that the architecture of the new building should include "the reestablishment of the baroque façades of the North, West and the South side, as well as the Schlüterhof courtyard of the former Berlin Palace".[1]

Respecting this decision, the project submitted to the 2008 competition for the "Reconstruction of the Berliner Schloss – Construction of the Humboldt Forum" was destined to conflict with some of the most deeply rooted ideological foundations of modern / contemporary architectural culture. In particular, with the idea that a reconstructed building cannot be authentic, even when it returns to its original place, and with the idea that the old form of a reconstructed façade is incom-

rekonstruierten Fassade nicht mit einer modernen Gestaltung und Funktion der Innenräume vereinbar sei.

Es erscheint mir sinnvoll, einige allgemeine Überlegungen zu diesen zentralen Themen des anhaltenden Streits der Ideen vorzustellen, der die Planung und Realisierung des Berliner Schlosses beziehungsweise des Humboldt Forums begleitet.

Mi è sembrato utile premettere alcune considerazioni generali su questi temi principali dell'ininterrotta battaglia delle idee che ha accompagnato la progettazione e la realizzazione del Berliner Schloss-Humboldt Forum.

patible with a modern configuration and function of the interior spaces.

I thought it's helpful to preface some general considerations on these main themes of the uninterrupted battle of ideas that accompanied the planning and realisation of the new Berliner Schloss-Humboldt Forum.

S. 22/23: Blick auf den neuen Spreeflügel und die rekonstruierte Nordfassade

P. 22/23: Veduta del nuovo edificio sulla Sprea e della ricostruita facciata nord

P. 22/23: View of the new building towards the Spree and the reconstructed north façade

Die Rekonstruktion
der zerstörten
Baudenkmäler

La ricostruzione
dei monumenti
distrutti

The reconstruction
of destroyed
monuments

Die Rekonstruktion
der zerstörten
Baudenkmäler

La ricostruzione
dei monumenti
distrutti

The reconstruction
of destroyed
monuments

Museumsinsel mit dem alten Schloss (oben)
und dem neuen Schloss (unten)

Isola dei Musei con il vecchio Castello (sopra)
e il nuovo Castello (sotto)

Museum Island with the old Palace (above)
and the new Palace (below)

Authentizität der Gebäude

Das neue Berliner Schloss – für die einen ein »modernes Gebäude mit barocken Fassaden«, für die anderen ein »barockes Gebäude mit einigen modernen Fassaden« – ist eine unmissverständliche Antwort auf die allgemeine Frage der Rekonstruktion von Gebäuden, die durch Gewalteinwirkung des Menschen oder der Natur zerstört wurden und die nicht durch originale Fragmente erfolgen kann, sondern lediglich mittels Zeichnungen, Beschreibungen und Fotografien.

Meines Erachtens muss bei der Frage nach der Authentizität einer Rekonstruktion die gleichsam ontologische Tatsache berücksichtigt werden, dass die Autoren der Entwürfe und der Bauausführungen sowie die entsprechenden Zeiträume nie dieselben sind.

Im Gegensatz zum Maler, der malt, was er sich vorstellt, oder zum Schriftsteller, der schreibt, was er denkt, entwirft der Architekt, baut aber nicht das Werk, das er mit seinem Entwurf antizipiert hat.

Autenticità degli edifici

Il nuovo Berliner Schloss – per alcuni «un edificio moderno con facciate barocche» e per altri «un edificio barocco con alcune facciate moderne» – rappresenta un'inequivocabile risposta alla più generale questione della ricostruzione degli edifici distrutti dall'azione violenta dell'uomo o della natura, quando essa non può darsi come ricomposizione dei loro frammenti, ma solo sulla base di disegni, descrizioni e fotografie.

Ritengo che l'autenticità di una ricostruzione si fondi, quasi ontologicamente, sul fatto che gli autori e i tempi del progetto e quelli della costruzione non sono mai gli stessi.

Diversamente dal pittore che dipinge ciò che si immagina, o dallo scrittore che scrive ciò che pensa, l'architetto progetta ma non costruisce l'opera prefigurata dal suo progetto.

La questione dell'autenticità di una ricostruzione si pone dunque in termini sostanzialmente simili a

Authenticity of buildings

The new Berlin Palace – for some a "modern building with baroque façades" and for others a "baroque building with some modern façades" – is an unequivocal answer to the more general question of reconstruction of buildings destroyed by man's or nature's violent action, when this cannot be done as a recomposition of their fragments, but only on the basis of drawings, descriptions and photographs.

I believe that the authenticity of a reconstruction is based, almost ontologically, on the fact that the authors and the times of the project and those of the construction are never the same.

Unlike the painter who paints what he imagines, or the writer who writes what he thinks, the architect plans but does not build the work prefigured by his project.

Therefore the conditions of authenticity of a reconstruction are substantially similar to those of the construction we define as original respect to the project. A thousand

Blick von Unter den Linden auf die
rekonstruierten Nord- und Westfassaden

Veduta da Unter den Linden delle ricostruite
facciate nord e ovest

View from Unter den Linden to the
reconstructed north and west façades

| Die Rekonstruktion der zerstörten Baudenkmäler | La ricostruzione dei monumenti distrutti | The reconstruction of destroyed monuments |

Die Frage der Authentizität einer Rekonstruktion stellt sich also im Wesentlichen unter den gleichen Bedingungen wie die der Konstruktion, die wir, gegenüber dem Entwurf, als Original bezeichnen. Tausende Gebäude, die an derselben Stelle und in der identischen Form des verschwundenen Gebäudes errichtet wurden, zeugen davon, dass die Rekonstruktion schon immer eine weit verbreitete Praxis in der europäischen Stadt war. Bis zum Beginn des letzten Jahrhunderts war sie eine der möglichen konfliktfreien Antworten auf die Frage, was man mit einem zerstörten Gebäude tun sollte.

Die berühmte Formel *dov'era e com'era* (wo es war und wie es war), die von der politischen Behörde für die Durchsetzung der Rekonstruktion des 1902 eingestürzten Campanile di San Marco in Venedig ausgesprochen wurde, weist nicht auf die Geburt der Rekonstruktion, sondern auf den Konflikt mit dem kurz zuvor erhobenen Architektenanspruch auf eine durch die jüngst erfundenen technischen Mittel erneuerte Form.[2]

quelli della costruzione che definiamo originale rispetto al progetto. Mille edifici che replicano forma e luogo di un edificio scomparso, testimoniano che la ricostruzione è sempre stata una pratica ovunque diffusa anche nella città europea. Fin quasi all'inizio del secolo scorso è stata una delle pacifiche risposte possibili al che fare di un edificio distrutto.

La famosa formula *dov'era e com'era*, pronunciata nel 1902 dall'autorità politica per imporre la ricostruzione del crollato Campanile di San Marco di Venezia, non è il certificato di nascita della ricostruzione, ma piuttosto del suo conflitto con la pretesa degli architetti di una forma rinnovata dai nuovi mezzi tecnici.[2]

L'opposizione alla ricostruzione è stata ed è tuttora sostenuta da due richieste contradditorie: da quella della 'materia originale' come condizione necessaria per l'autenticità di un antico edificio e da quella della 'forma originale' come condizione necessaria per l'autenticità di un nuovo edificio.

buildings replicating the form in the same place of a lost building testify to the fact that reconstruction has always been a widespread practice, even in the European city. Since almost the beginning of the last century, it has been one of the peaceful possible answers to what to do with a destroyed building.

The famous formula *dov'era e com'era* (where it was and how it was), pronounced in 1902 by the political authority to impose the reconstruction of the collapsed Campanile di San Marco in Venice, is not explained by the birth of reconstruction, but rather of its conflict with the architects' claim to a form renewed by new technical means.[2]

The opposition to reconstruction was and still is sustained by two contradictory claims: that of the 'original material' as a necessary condition for the authenticity of an old building and that of the 'original form' as a condition for the authenticity of a new building.

John Ruskin's "traces of age", Alois Riegl's "value of age", or Georg

Blick auf den neuen Spreeflügel und
die rekonstruierte Nordfassade

Veduta del nuovo edificio sulla Sprea e
della ricostruita facciata nord

View of the new building towards the Spree
and the reconstructed north façade

Der Rekonstruktion hielt man damals wie heute zwei einander widersprechende Anforderungen entgegen: Bedingung für die Authentizität eines alten Gebäudes ist die ›originale Bausubstanz‹, für die Authentizität eines neuen Gebäudes die ›originale Form‹.

John Ruskins »Altersspuren«, Alois Riegls »Alterswert«, Georg Dehios »konservieren, nicht restaurieren«: Diese weithin bekannten Begriffe und Thesen vom Ende des 19. und Anfang des 20. Jahrhunderts setzten sich in der Theorie und Praxis der Denkmalpflege und der Restaurierung durch und sind auch heute noch von entscheidender Bedeutung.

Nachdem zunächst die *stilistische Restaurierung* in der Manier Viollet-le-Ducs ins Visier genommen worden war, die selbst ohne hinreichende Dokumentation partielle und komplette Rekonstruktionen und sogar neue Konstruktionen im romanisch-gotischen Stil billigte, erstreckte sich das Aburteil bald auch auf die genau dokumentierte Rekon-

«Le tracce dell'età» di John Ruskin, il «valore dell'età» di Alois Riegl, o il «conservare e non restaurare» di Georg Dehio: queste tesi ben note, enunciate nel tardo Ottocento/inizi Novecento, si imposero nella dottrina e nella pratica della Conservazione e Restauro, conservando fino ad oggi un'importanza decisiva.

Dal primo bersaglio polemico – il *restauro stilistico* alla maniera di Viollet-le-Duc, che consentiva, anche in assenza della necessaria documentazione, la ricostruzione, il completamento o addirittura la costruzione di nuovi edifici in stile romanico-gotico – la condanna si è estesa presto alla ricostruzione ampiamente documentata: anch'essa viene accusata di essere un falso storico e dunque una costruzione non autentica, anche se nel frattempo il rilievo fotogrammetrico, introdotto nell'architettura verso la fine dell'Ottocento, era in grado di restituire la fisionomia di un edificio con la stessa precisione dei disegni del progetto originale.

Dehio's "conserve and not restore": these well-known theses, enunciated in the late 19th/early 20th century, became established in the doctrine and practice of Conservation and Restoration and remain of decisive importance to this day.

From the first polemical target – the *stylistic restoration* in the manner of Viollet-le-Duc, which allowed, even in the absence of the necessary documentation, the reconstruction, completion or even construction of new buildings in Romanesque-Gothic style – the condemnation was soon extended to the widely documented reconstruction, also accused of being a historical fake and therefore a not authentic construction, even though in the meantime photogrammetric surveying, which was introduced in architecture towards the end of the 19th century, was capable of rendering the physiognomy of a building with the same precision as the original design drawings.

This accuse seems to be based on the organicistic idea that a building, like the human body, can be healed

Blick auf den neuen Spreeflügel und
das rekonstruierte Eckturm-Rondell

Veduta del nuovo edificio sulla Sprea e
della ricostruita torretta d'angolo-Rondell

View of the new building towards the Spree
and the reconstructed corner turret-Rondell

struktion: Sie wurde als historische Fälschung und damit als eine nicht authentische Konstruktion angeprangert, obwohl die fotogrammetrische Vermessung, die gegen Ende des 19. Jahrhunderts in die Architektur eingeführt wurde, die Physiognomie eines Gebäudes ebenso präzise wiedergeben kann wie die originalen Entwurfspläne.

Dieses Aburteil scheint auf der organizistischen Vorstellung zu beruhen, dass ein Gebäude wie der menschliche Körper geheilt werden kann, wenn es krank ist, aber wenn es tot ist, nicht wieder auferstehen kann. Als ob im Falle der Zerstörung seines (Bau)Körpers auch seine ›Seele‹ beziehungsweise seine Bedeutung unwiederbringlich verlorengehen würde. Im Gegensatz zum Menschen, dessen ›Seele‹ sich in einem sich ständig verändernden Körper erhält, wird ein Gebäude stets mit seiner Körperform identifiziert, das heißt mit etwas, das prinzipiell immer reproduziert werden kann. Das ›Organische‹ stellt die Grenzlinie dar zwischen reproduzierbaren und nicht reprodu-

Un'accusa che sembra fondarsi sull'idea organicistica che un edificio, analogamente al corpo umano, possa essere risanato quando è ammalorato, ma non risuscitato quando è morto. Come se, nel caso della distruzione del suo corpo, anche la sua 'anima' - ovvero la sua importanza per noi e chi verrà dopo di noi - andasse irrimediabilmente perduta. Diversamente dall'uomo, la cui 'anima' abita in un corpo sempre mutevole, un edificio si identifica con la forma del suo corpo, ovvero con qualcosa che, in linea di principio, può essere sempre riprodotta. L''organico' definisce, io penso, la linea di demarcazione fra le cose riproducibili e irriproducibili: rispettivamente fra il mondo del non-organico, a cui appartengono anche gli edifici, e quello dell'organico di alberi, animali e uomini.

La riproduzione di una determinata forma con l'impiego di nuova materia riguarda pressoché tutti gli edifici antichi ancora in uso, anche quelli che non classifichiamo come

when it is sick, but not resurrected when it is dead. As if, in the case of the destruction of its body, its 'soul' – that is, its importance for us and for those who will come after us – is also irretrievably lost.

Unlike man, whose 'soul' dwells in an ever-changing body, a building is identified with the form of its body, i.e. with something that, in principle, can always be reproduced. The 'organic' defines, I think, the dividing line between reproducible and irreproducible things: respectively between the world of the non-organic, to which buildings also belong, and the organic world of trees, animals and humans.

The reproduction of a certain form using new material concerns almost all ancient buildings still in use, even those that we do not classify as reconstruction. Most of the material that our eyes can see – for example plasters, windows, roof coverings – has also been partly or completely replaced several times over the course of time. Yet we still perceive them as authentic, just as the Athe-

Das Portal I der rekonstruierten Südfassade

Il Portale I della ricostruita facciata sud

The Portal I of the reconstructed south façade

zierbaren Dingen beziehungsweise zwischen der Welt des Nichtorganischen, zu der auch Gebäude gehören, und derjenigen des Organischen, der Bäume, Tiere und Menschen.

Die Reproduktion einer bestehenden Form unter Verwendung von neuem Material ist ein Sachverhalt, der auf fast alle alten Gebäude zutrifft. Der größte Teil der materiellen Substanz – Putz, Fenster, Dacheindeckungen –, wurde im Laufe der Zeit mehrmals in Teilen oder sogar vollständig ersetzt. Dennoch halten wir die Gebäude weiterhin für authentisch, so wie die Athener vor dreitausend Jahren davon überzeugt waren, dass das legendäre Schiff des Theseus das *wahre* Schiff des Theseus sei, auch wenn all seine hölzernen Bestandteile eines nach dem anderen, unter Bewahrung ihrer jeweiligen Form, ausgetauscht worden waren. Plutarch berichtet: »Das Schiff, auf dem Theseus die Überfahrt gemacht hatte und das mit den jungen Männern sicher zurückgekehrt war, ein Schiff mit dreißig Rudern, bewahrten die Athener bis zur Zeit des

ricostruzione. La maggior parte della materia che i nostri occhi possono vedere – ad esempio gli intonaci, le finestre, il rivestimento dei tetti – è stata anche più volte sostituita in parte o del tutto nel corso del tempo. Eppure noi continuiamo a percepire quegli edifici come autentici, così come gli Ateniesi di tremila anni fa ritenevano che la leggendaria nave di Teseo fosse la vera nave di Teseo, anche quando i suoi legni, uno dopo l'altro, erano stati sostituiti, replicandone la forma.

Racconta Plutarco: «La nave sulla quale Teseo aveva compiuto la traversata ed era tornato indietro con i giovani sani e salvi, una nave a trenta remi, gli ateniesi la conservarono fino ai tempi di Demetrio Falereo [per più di mille anni, *n. d. s.*] eliminando le vecchie assi di legno, sostituendole con altre solide e inserendole in modo tale che per i filosofi la nave costituisse un buon esempio per ragionare sul discorso della crescita [dell'identità, *n. d. s.*]; c'è infatti chi sostiene che la nave sia rimasta la stessa, chi invece lo nega.»[3]

nians of three thousand years ago believed that the legendary ship of Theseus was the *true* ship of Theseus, even when its timbers, one after the other, had been replaced, replicating its shape.

Plutarch tells: "The ship on which Theseus had made his crossing and had returned safely with the young men, a ship with thirty oars, the Athenians preserved until the time of Demetrius Phalereus [more than a thousand years, *author's note*] by removing the old wooden planks, replacing them with solid ones and inserting them in such a way that for philosophers the ship was a good example to reason about the discourse of growth [of identity, *author's note*]; there are those who say that the ship has remained the same, those who deny it."[3]

A philosophical challenge not only for Plato and Aristotle, but also for philosophers much later. One of the best known 'denialist' arguments is based on the hypothesis, put forward by Thomas Hobbes in the 17th century, of the reconstruction of the

Das Portal V der rekonstruierten Nordfassade

Il Portale V della ricostruita facciata sud

The Portal V of the reconstructed south façade

Demetrius Phalereus [d. h. mehr als tausend Jahre lang, *Anm. d. Verf.*] auf, indem sie die alten Holzplanken entfernten, sie durch solide Planken ersetzten und sie so einfügten, dass das Schiff für die Philosophen als gutes Beispiel diente für ihren Disput über den Wandel [der Identität, *Anm. d. Verf.*] in der Veränderung der Dinge; es gibt welche, die behaupten, dass das Schiff dasselbe geblieben sei, und andere, die es leugnen.«[3]

Eine philosophische Herausforderung nicht nur für Platon und Aristoteles, sondern auch für die Philosophen der folgenden Jahrhunderte. Eines der bekanntesten Argumente ist die von Thomas Hobbes im 17. Jahrhundert aufgestellte These, das *echte* Theseus-Schiff könnte auch durch die Zusammensetzung der aufbewahrten alten Originalholzteile rekonstruiert worden sein. Diese Idee von der Authentizität der Objekte berücksichtigt allerdings nicht die Veränderung der Materie im Laufe der Zeit.

Ganz allgemein beruht die Ansicht, dass die Rekonstruktion eine

Una sfida filosofica non solo per Platone e Aristotele, ma anche per i filosofi di molto tempo successivi. Uno degli argomenti più noti dei 'negazionisti' si sostiene sull'ipotesi, prospettata da Thomas Hobbes nel 17° secolo, della ricostruzione della *vera* nave di Teseo attraverso la ricomposizione di tutti i suoi vecchi legni originali. E' un'idea dell'autenticità degli oggetti, che non tiene conto dell'alterazione della materia nel corso del tempo.

Più in generale la convinzione che la ricostruzione sia un falso storico si fonda sull'identificazione dell'edificio perduto con una astratta idea di originale, come qualcosa che compete solo alla 'prima costruzione'. Al contrario di quanto ancora dicono le direttive e raccomandazioni della Cura e Restauro dei Monumenti, ritengo che la ricostruzione possa essere intesa come una sorta di *ultima ratio* della Conservazione dell'Antico.

Di un difetto di autenticità della ricostruzione parlano anche le alternanti accuse di storicismo, postmo-

true Theseus' ship by reassembling all its original old timbers. It is an idea of the authenticity of objects, which does not consider the alteration of the material in the course of time.

More generally, the conviction that reconstruction is a historical fake is based on the identification of the lost building with an abstract idea of the original as something that belongs only to the 'first construction'. Contrary to what the guidelines and recommendations of the Care and Restoration of Monuments still say, I believe that reconstruction can be understood as a kind of *ultima ratio* for the Conservation of Antiquity.

Even the alternating accusations of historicism, post-modernism or antimodern-conservatism', levelled by architects who believe that only an original Form can be representative of the *spirit of the times*, speak of a defect of authenticity of the reconstruction. Underlying these objections is a fundamentalist idea of the New, which not only opposes the reconstruction of the Old, but has

Blick auf die rekonstruierte Nordfassade

Veduta della ricostruita facciata nord

View of the reconstructed north façade

historische Fälschung sei, auf der Identifizierung des verlorenen Gebäudes mit einer abstrakten Idee des Originals, das nur mit der ersten Errichtung (›ersten Konstruktion‹) übereinstimmt. Im Gegensatz zu den heute tonangebenden Richtlinien beziehungsweise Empfehlungen zur Restaurierung und Denkmalpflege halte ich die Rekonstruktion für die *ultima ratio* der Konservierung von alten Bauwerken.

Auf einen Mangel an Authentizität weisen auch die Vorwürfe des Historismus, Postmodernismus oder antimodernen Konservatismus hin, die von Architekten geäußert werden, für die nur die originelle Form dem *Zeitgeist* angemessen ist. Grundlage dieser Vorwürfe ist eine fundamentalistische Idee des Neuen, die sich nicht nur der Rekonstruktion des Alten widersetzt, sondern wiederholt dessen Existenz selbst in Frage gestellt hat.

In den 1920er und 1930er Jahren plädierten Architekten wie Le Corbusier oder Hilberseimer für eine *tabula rasa* in den zentralen Bereichen

dernismo, conservatorismo-antimoderno, ad essa rivolte da parte degli architetti che ritengono che solo una Forma originale possa essere rappresentativa dello *spirito del tempo*. Alla base di queste accuse c'è un'idea fondamentalistica del Nuovo, che non solo si oppone alla ricostruzione dell'Antico, ma che ha più volte contraddetto la sua stessa esistenza.

Ad esempio: negli anni Venti-Trenta del secolo scorso Le Corbusier o Hilberseimer prevedevano la *tabula rasa* nelle aree centrali di Parigi o nella Friedrichstadt e nella Altstadt di Berlino come ideale banco di prova di una radicale città contemporanea, che poteva essere costruita dovunque, sempre uguale a sé stessa. Un'idea analoga ha ispirato, nei primi decenni del Dopoguerra, la cancellazione della struttura urbana e dell'edificazione di numerose aree centrali, non solo di quelle devastate dagli eventi bellici.

Anche l'odierna opposizione alla ricostruzione è spesso sostenuta da promesse di progresso sociale e tecnico, simili a quelle già più volte spe-

repeatedly contradicted its own existence.

For example: in the 1920s and 1930s Le Corbusier or Hilberseimer envisaged the *tabula rasa* in the central areas of Paris or in Friedrichstadt and Altstadt of Berlin as an ideal test-bed for a radical contemporary city, which could be built anywhere, always the same. A similar idea inspired, in the first decades of the post-war period, the cancellation of the urban structure and the building of many central areas, not only those devastated by the war events.

Even today's opposition to reconstruction is often underpinned by promises of social and technical progress, similar to those already experienced many times before with mediocre, if not bad urban and architectural results.

Each time overcoming the opposition of the 'avantgardistic New' and the 'authentic Old', the reconstruction of monuments and entire districts of the European city, destroyed by two world wars or natural disasters, has been widely practised.

Blick auf die rekonstruierte Südfassade

Veduta della ricostruita facciata sud

View of the reconstructed south façade

von Paris oder Berlin. Sie sahen sie als ideales Versuchsfeld für eine radikal zeitgenössische Stadt, die überall immer gleich sein sollte. Eine ähnliche Idee inspirierte in der Nachkriegszeit die Auflösung zentraler Stadtteile, nicht nur der im Krieg zerstörten. Noch heute wird die Kritik an der Rekonstruktion häufig mit Verheißungen eines Fortschritts vorgetragen, die bereits mehrfach zu mediokren architektonischen Ergebnissen führten. Die immer wieder aufgetretene Opposition des ›zukunftweisenden Neuen‹ und des ›authentischen‹ Alten wurde durch die Rekonstruktion zahlreicher Baudenkmäler bis hin zu ganzen Stadtvierteln mehrmals überwunden. In Deutschland wurden die meisten im Laufe des Zweiten Weltkriegs zerstörten Residenzschlösser wiederhergestellt, in Berlin die wichtigsten Gebäude und Plätze, die auf das Stadtschloss Bezug nahmen. Die Identität vieler historischer Stadtzentren Europas ist zu einem gewichtigen Teil der Rekonstruktion zu verdanken.

rimentate con mediocri, se non pessimi risultati urbani e architettonici.

Ogni volta superando un'opposizione in nome del 'Nuovo avanguardistico' e dell''Antico autentico', la ricostruzione dei monumenti e di interi quartieri della città europea, distrutti da due guerre mondiali o da catastrofi naturali, è stata ampiamente praticata. In particolare in Germania, sono stati ricostruiti i castelli-residenza distrutti nel corso della seconda guerra mondiale, e, a Berlino, i principali edifici e luoghi pubblici in origine riferiti al Castello di città degli Hohenzollern.

Penso si possa dire che l'identità di numerosi centri storici della città europea dipenda in non trascurabile misura dalla ricostruzione.

In particular, over the past seventy years, numerous palaces-residences in the German city have been reconstructed, and, in Berlin, the main buildings and public places originally referred to the Hohenzollern City Palace.

I think it can be said that the preservation of the identity of many historic European city centres, depends to no small extent on reconstruction.

Blick auf die rekonstruierten West- und Südfassaden

Veduta delle ricostruite facciate ovest e sud

View of the reconstructed west and south façades

Einmaligkeit des Ortes

Auf der Nichtreproduzierbarkeit des Ortes, seiner materiellen und immateriellen Besonderheiten, gründet sich der wesentliche Unterschied zwischen Rekonstruktion und Kopie: zwischen dem Gebäude, das den Platz eines anderen, nicht mehr existierenden einnimmt, dessen Form es nachbildet, und den unzähligen Gebäuden, die die Form eines nicht mehr existierenden, aber auch eines noch existierenden Gebäudes anderswo wiederholen können.

Dabei spielt es keine Rolle, ob eine Kopie vor oder nach der eigentlichen Rekonstruktion entstanden ist, und ebenso wenig, ob Teile des zerstörten Gebäudes in der Kopie wiederverwendet wurden. Beim Berliner Schloss wird der architektonisch-städtebauliche Wert des originalgetreu rekonstruierten Portals IV durch die Kopie, die in das nahegelegene ehemalige Staatsratsgebäude eingefügt wurde, in keiner Weise geschmälert, selbst wenn diese mehrere Fragmente des Originalportals aufweist.

Unicità del Luogo

Sulla non riproducibiltà del Luogo, delle sue peculiarità materiali e immateriali, si fonda la sostanziale differenza fra la ricostruzione e la copia: fra quell'unico edificio che può prendere il posto di un'altro, replicandone la forma, e gli innumerevoli edifici, con la stessa forma di un altro, ancora o non più esistente, che si possono costruire altrove.

Non importa se la copia viene prima o dopo la ricostruzione, né l'eventuale reimpiego nella copia di frammenti dell'edificio distrutto. Nel caso del Castello di Berlino, il valore architettonico-urbano del Portale IV, ricostruito in maniera il più possibile fedele all'originale, non viene affatto sminuito dall'esistenza della sua copia, pur arricchita da alcuni frammenti del portale originale, inserita nel vicino edificio dell'ex Staatsratsgebäude.

Dati i mezzi tecnici del nostro tempo, anche nel caso della pittura il criterio del Luogo può essere più importante di quello della Materia:

Uniqueness of the Place

The substantial difference between reconstruction and copy is based on the non-reproducibility of the place, of its material and immaterial peculiarities: between that only one building that can take the place of another replicating its form, and the innumerable buildings that can be built elsewhere, with the same form as another, still or no longer existing.

It is not important if the copy was made before or after the reconstruction, nor if fragments of the destroyed building were reused in the copy. In the case of Berlin Palace, the architectural-urban value of the Portal IV, reconstructed as faithfully as possible to the original, is in no way diminished by the existence of its copy, enriched by same fragments of the original portal, inserted into the near building of the former Staatsratsgebäude.

Due to the technical means of our time, even in the case of painting, the criterion of the original Place may be more important than that of the

Ansicht des rekonstruierten Eckturm-Rondells
Veduta della ricostruita torretta d'angolo-Rondell
View of the reconstructed corner turret-Rondell

Die Rekonstruktion der zerstörten Baudenkmäler	La ricostruzione dei monumenti distrutti	The reconstruction of destroyed monuments

Aufgrund der technischen Mittel unserer Zeit kann der Ort sogar in der Malerei wichtiger sein als die materielle Substanz: Die perfekte Kopie des großen Gemäldes *Le Nozze di Cana* (Die Hochzeit zu Kana) von Paolo Veronese, die an den Ort zurückgekehrt ist, für den es bestimmt war – eine Wand des palladianischen Refektoriums des Klosters San Giorgio in Venedig –, ist in kunsthistorisch-kultureller Hinsicht bedeutsamer als das von Napoleon geraubte Original, das im Louvre ausgestellt wird.

Der Begriff des Ortes ist meines Erachtens auf den urbanen Kontext des Gebäudes auszudehnen. Das Berliner Schloss kehrt eben nicht nur an seinen ursprünglichen Ort, sondern auch in seinen architektonisch-stadträumlichen Kontext zurück, also zu den wichtigsten, größtenteils rekonstruierten Gebäuden und Plätzen des monumentalen historischen Zentrums von Berlin.

Die Gleichsetzung von Rekonstruktion und Kopie, die heute von Architekten oft selbstverständlich

la copia perfetta della grande tela *Le nozze di Cana* di Paolo Veronese, esposta nel luogo per il quale era stata pensata e a lungo era stata – il palladiano Refettorio del Convento di San Giorgio a Venezia – è più ricca di significato culturale/storico-artistico di quella originale, trafugata da Napoleone e ora esposta al Louvre.

La nozione di Luogo è da estendere, a mio avviso, al contesto urbano dell'edificio. Il Castello di Berlino ritorna non solo nel luogo, ma anche nel contesto architettonico e dello spazio pubblico in cui si trovava, ovvero fra i principali edifici e luoghi del centro storico-monumentale di Berlino, anch'essi in gran parte ricostruiti.

Ritengo che l'equivalenza di ricostruzione e copia, oggi spesso data per scontata anche dagli architetti, sia un sintomo della perdita di importanza del luogo, e quindi del valore urbano dell'architettura.

Il *luogo*, non la materia e la sua forma, oggi quasi sempre riproducibili, fa la differenza fra l'unica copia

original material. The perfect copy of Paolo Veronese's large painting *Le Nozze di Cana* (The Wedding at Cana), exposed in the place for which it was intended and in which for a long time it was – the Palladian Refectory of the Convent of San Giorgio in Venice – is richer in artistic-historical significance than the original one, stolen by Napoleon and now exposed in the Louvre.

The notion of Place is to be extended, I believe, to the urban context of the building. The Berlin Palace returns not only to its site, but also to the architectural and public space context in which it was located, i.e. among the main buildings and public spaces of Berlin's historical and monumental centre, also in large part reconstructed.

I think that the equivalence of reconstruction and copy, which is often taken for granted today even by architects, is a symptom of the loss of importance of the place, and therefore of the urban value of architecture.

The *place*, not the material and its form which today are almost al-

Schlüterhof
Blick von der Terrasse im zweiten Geschoss
Veduta dalla terrazza del secondo piano
View from the second floor terrace

betrieben wird, ist meines Erachtens ein Zeichen für den Bedeutungsverlust des Ortes und damit des urbanen Werts der Architektur.

Der *Ort*, nicht das Material oder die Form, die heute fast immer reproduzierbar sind, macht – auch im Hinblick auf die Authentizität – den wesentlichen Unterschied zwischen der einzig möglichen Rekonstruktion eines ortsfesten, immobilen Objekts (eines Gebäudes) und den unzähligen Kopien der mobilen Objekte des Industriedesigns aus.

possibile di un oggetto-immobile, ovvero di un edificio, e le innumerevoli copie possibili degli oggetti-mobili dell'industrial design.

ways reproducible, makes the difference between the only possible copy of an immobile-object, i.e. a building, and the innumerable possible copies of the mobile-objects of industrial design.

Blick auf die rekonstruierte Nordfassade

Veduta della ricostruita facciata sud

View of the reconstructed south façade

Identität der Fassade

Von allen Elementen eines Gebäudes ist die Fassade die bevorzugte Zielscheibe der Kritik an der Rekonstruktion. Insbesondere wenn, wie im Fall des Berliner Schlosses, die ›alte‹ Form der Fassade mit einer modernen Gestaltung und Funktion der Innenräume korrespondiert. Dabei wird übersehen, dass die Fassaden vieler der bedeutenden Gebäude in der europäischen Stadt von prestigeträchtigen Vorbildern der Architekturgeschichte und nicht von den Innenräumen inspiriert wurden. Als Ausdruck der Würde eines Gebäudes und als Schmuckelement der Stadt wurde die Fassade lange als *Kunstwerk per se* betrachtet, dem sowohl die schon existierenden als auch die noch nicht entworfenen Räume dahinter angepasst werden sollten.

Der besondere urbane Wert der Fassade wurde schon um die Mitte des 15. Jahrhunderts von Leon Battista Alberti behandelt: »[…] da wir unsere Häuser zu schmücken gewohnt sind, […] ist es zweifellos erstrebens-

Identità della Facciata

Fra tutti gli elementi di un edificio, la facciata è il bersaglio preferito dall'opposizione ideologica alla ricostruzione, soprattutto quando, come nel caso del Berliner Schloss, alla sua antica forma corrisponde una moderna configurazione e funzione degli spazi interni. Si dimentica il fatto che la forma della facciata di numerosi fra i più importanti edifici della città europea, è stata ispirata dai modelli più prestigiosi della storia dell'architettura, assai più che dallo spazio interno. In quanto espressione della dignità dell'edificio e del decoro della città, la facciata è stata a lungo considerata come *opera d'arte di per sé*, a cui dovevano adattarsi le case retrostanti, sia quelle preesistenti sia quelle non ancora progettate.

Il particolare valore urbano della facciata fu ben riconosciuto già verso la metà del 15° secolo da Leon Battista Alberti: «[…] poiché siamo soliti adornare le nostre case […] la cosa migliore sarà indubbia-

Identity of the Façade

Of all the elements of a building, the façade is the preferred target of ideological opposition to reconstruction, especially when, as in the case of the Berlin Palace, to its old form corresponds a modern configuration and function of the interior spaces. One forgets the fact that the form of the façade of many of the most important buildings in the European city has been inspired by the most prestigious models in the history of architecture, far more than by the interior space. As expression of the dignity of the building and the decorum of the city, the façade has long been regarded as a *work of art in itself*, to which the houses behind had to be adapted, both those existing and those not yet planned.

The particular urban value of the façade was already recognised in the mid-15th century by Leon Battista Alberti: "[…] since we are used to adorning our houses […] the best thing will undoubtedly be to ensure that those parts of the building that

Blick auf die rekonstruierte Kuppel

Veduta della cupola ricostruita

View of the reconstructed dome

wert, dass jene Gebäudeteile, die eine größere öffentliche Sichtbarkeit haben – wie die Fassade, das Atrium usw. –, besonders reich verziert sein sollten.«[4]

Das erklärt, warum die Fassade vom 15. bis ins späte 19. Jahrhundert das vorrangige Thema der öffentlichen Kontrolle von Architektur war. Nicht selten war sie so stark, dass sich die Konstruktion von besonders repräsentativen Straßen und Plätzen aus der Addition eines vorgeschriebenen Fassadenmoduls ergab: Üblicherweise war dessen Entwurf einem berühmten Architekten anvertraut, und die jeweiligen Eigentümer der dahinterliegenden Häuser waren zur Ausführung verpflichtet.

Auch die rekonstruierte Fassade des Berliner Schlosses lässt sich viel besser durch den Verweis auf ihre architektonischen Vorbilder als durch die Konfiguration und Funktion der Innenräume erklären: Zu nennen sind die antiken römischen Triumphbögen, die ideale Piazza und die Stadttore der Renaissance, die auf Michelangelo zurückgehende Kom-

mente provvedere affinché riescano quanto più possibile decorose quelle parti dell'edificio che più sono a contatto con il pubblico, come è il caso della facciata, del vestibolo, etc.»[4]

Questo spiega perché dal 15° al tardo 19° secolo sia stata il luogo privilegiato del controllo pubblico dell'architettura. Un controllo non di rado così forte da dettare la costruzione di strade e piazze particolarmente rappresentative attraverso l'addizione di uno stesso modulo di facciata, il cui progetto veniva di solito affidato a qualche famoso architetto, mentre la sua realizzazione era a carico dei diversi proprietari delle case retrostanti.

Anche il disegno della facciata ricostruita del Castello di Berlino si può spiegare, meglio che con la configurazione e funzione degli spazi interni, con i modelli architettonici che l'hanno ispirata: gli antichi archi trionfali romani, la Piazza ideale e la Porta di Città del Rinascimento, la michelangiolesca combinazione dell'ordine gigante con il

are most in contact with the public, such as the façade, the vestibule, etc., are as decorative as possible."[4]

This explains why from the 15th to the late 19th century, it was the privileged place of public control of architecture. This control was often so strong that it dictated the construction of particularly representative streets and squares through the addition of the same façade module, whose project was usually commited to famous architects, and then the owners of the houses behind had to build it.

Even the design of the reconstructed façade of Berlin Palace can be explained, better than by the configuration and function of the interior spaces, by the architectural models that inspired it: for example, by the ancient Roman triumphal arches, the Ideal Piazza and the Town Gate of the Renaissance, the Michelangelo's combination of the giant order with the simple one, or by vertical partition of the storeys, friezes and cornices of the Palazzo Madama in Rome.

Das rekonstruierte Nordportal der neuen Passage

Il ricostruito Portale nord del nuovo Passage

The reconstructed north Portal of the new Passage

bination aus Kolossal- und eingeschossiger Ordnung sowie die Geschossgliederungen, Friese und Gesimse des Palazzo Madama in Rom.

Das mangelnde Interesse an der urbanen Bedeutung der Fassade geht auf die Abtrennung der Gebäudearchitektur vom Städtebau zurück, die in der Moderne erfolgte, auf die ›Befreiung‹ oder Emanzipation des Gebäudes von der traditionellen Aufgabe, Teil der Straße oder des Platzes zu sein und damit einen Beitrag zur Schönheit der Stadt zu leisten. Es handelt sich um eine Revolution in der Rangordnung der Bauelemente und der Perspektiven: Der Blick von der Stadt auf das Haus weicht dem Blick von innen aus dem Haus nach außen. Der Vorrang der Fassade, dem Ort der Allgemeinheit, wird dem Gebäudeinneren gegeben, das mit wenigen Ausnahmen ein Ort der privaten Nutzung ist.

In Berlin zeigt die aktuelle Debatte um die Rekonstruktion der Bauakademie, dass in der architektonischen Kultur noch immer eine ideologische Position gegen die Fas-

normale ordine di piano, o la partizione dei piani, i fregi e le cornici del romano Palazzo Madama.

Lo scarso interesse per il valore urbano della facciata dipende dal moderno divorzio del progetto dell'edificio da quello della città, dalla 'liberazione' dell'architettura dell'edificio dal tradizionale compito di essere un pezzo di strada o di piazza, di pubblica utilità e bellezza. Si tratta di una rivoluzione della gerarchia di valore dei caratteri edilizi e dei punti di vista: quello dall'interno della casa all'esterno si impone su quello dalla città alla casa, e al primato della facciata – luogo pubblico della possibile esperienza di tutti – succede quello dello spazio interno – con poche eccezioni, luogo dell'esperienza dei suoi soli utilizzatori.

A Berlino, l'attuale dibattito sulla ricostruzione della Bauakademie mostra la persistenza di un rapporto ideologico della cultura architettonica con la facciata. Come si poteva facilmente immaginare, è fallito il tentativo, perseguito attraverso due

The loss of interest in the urban value of the façade depends on the modern divorce of the design of the building from that of the city, on the 'liberation' of the architecture of the building from the traditional purpose of being a piece of street or square, of public utility and beauty. It is a revolution in the hierarchy of value of the building characters and points of view: that from inside the house to the outside imposes itself on that from the city to the house, and the primacy of the façade, the public place of everyone's possible experience, is succeeded by that of the interior space – with a few exceptions, the place of the experience of its users alone.

In today's Berlin, the debate on the reconstruction of the Bauakademie shows the persistence of an ideological relationship of architectural culture to the façade. As one could easily imagine, the attempt, pursued through two successive competitions, to solve the question of the façade through a preliminary definition and function of the interior

Das rekonstruierte Portal des Schlüterhofs

Il ricostruito Portale della corte Schlüterhof

The reconstructed Portal of the courtyard Schlüterhof

sade bezogen wird. Leicht hätte man sich ausrechnen können, dass der in zwei aufeinanderfolgenden Wettbewerben unternommene Versuch scheitern würde, die Frage der Fassade durch die Festlegung der Funktion der Innenräume zu lösen. Der Grund für diesen Misserfolg liegt meines Erachtens in der zu wenig beachteten und respektierten Tatsache, dass die von Schinkel entworfene Fassade nicht nur der gelegentlichen und wechselnden Funktion des Gebäudes, sondern vor allem dauerhaft der Schönheit der Stadt dienen sollte: In diesem Sinn ist sie ein *Kunstwerk per se*, dessen originalgetreue Rekonstruktion uns vieles über die Geschichte der Architektur und der Stadt Berlin mitteilen kann.

Auch Schinkel, der Architekt der Bauakademie, wurde von denen ›rekrutiert‹, die für eine neue, dem *Zeitgeist* entsprechende Fassade plädieren. Zugegeben, nicht nur Schinkel, sondern auch die Architekten der griechischen und römischen Antike, der Gotik und der Renaissance bis zu den Vertretern der Moderne des letz-

successivi concorsi, di risolvere la questione della facciata attraverso una preliminare definizione e funzione dello spazio interno. All'origine di questo fallimento è il disconoscimento del fatto che la facciata disegnata da Schinkel è stata pensata in funzione di una duratura bellezza della città oltreché per l'occasionale, cangiante destinazione d'uso dell' edificio: in questo senso essa è un' *opera d'arte di per sé*, la cui ricostruzione può dirci ancor molto di interessante sulla storia dell'architettura in generale e sulla città di Berlino.

Anche Schinkel, l'architetto della Bauakademie, è stato 'arruolato' nel partito di coloro che auspicano una forma nuova, rappresentativa dello *spirito del tempo*. Ammettiamolo pure: non solo Schinkel, ma neanche gli architetti dell'antica Grecia e Roma, del Gotico e del Rinascimento, e così via, fino ai moderni del secolo scorso, rifarebbero oggi quello che hanno fatto al loro tempo. Che cosa significa tutto ciò? Che il Passato deve cedere il posto al Presente, e quest'ultimo presto al Fu-

space failed. Cause of this failure is the disavowal of the fact that the façade designed by Schinkel was conceived for the lasting beauty of the city as well as for the occasional use of the building: in this sense it is a *work of art in itself*, whose reconstruction can still tell us much of interest about the history of architecture in general and the city of Berlin.

Even Schinkel, the architect of the Bauakademie, has been 'enlisted' in the party of those who advocate a new form, representative of the *spirit of the time*. Let's admit it: not only Schinkel, but not even the architects of ancient Greece and Rome, of the Gothic and the Renaissance, and so on, up to many moderns of the last century, would not do today what they did in their time. What does this mean? That the Past should give way to the Present, which in turn will soon be replaced by a Future? Why then not also call for the removal of Schinkel's still existing buildings?

In the case of the Berlin Palace, the accusation of historicism or passatism comes from those who think

Foyer

Blick vom Atrium des rekonstruierten
Portals III auf die Loggien des Foyers

Veduta dei loggiati del Foyer dall'atrio
del ricostruito Portale III

View of the loggias of the Foyer from the
atrium of the reconstructed Portal III

ten Jahrhunderts würden heute nicht mehr so bauen wie zu ihrer Zeit. Was bedeutet das? Dass die Vergangenheit der Gegenwart und diese wiederum der Zukunft weichen muss? Warum nicht gleich auch die noch existierenden Bauten Schinkels beseitigen?

Im Fall des Berliner Schlosses kommt der Vorwurf des Fassadismus von denjenigen, die der Fassade keine eigenständige urbane Bedeutung beimessen. Doch im kollektiven Gedächtnis wird das Berliner Schloss mit der barocken Fassade gleichgesetzt, und das rechtfertigt mein Einverständnis mit der Entscheidung des Deutschen Bundestages, der Rekonstruktion der Baukörper-Stereometrie, der barocken Fassade sowie der Kuppel aus dem 19. Jahrhundert Priorität einzuräumen.

Eine umfassende, auf sorgfältiger Recherche beruhende Dokumentation ermöglichte eine originalgetreue und daher authentische Rekonstruktion aller Bauteile, sowohl der von der Politik vorgegebenen als auch der von meinem Entwurf hinzugefügten.

turo? Perché allora non auspicare anche la rimozione degli edifici di Schinkel tuttora esistenti?

Nel caso del Castello di Berlino, l'accusa di storicismo o passatismo proviene da chi pensa che la facciata non abbia di per sé alcuna importanza civile e urbana, trascurando il fatto che esso, nella memoria collettiva, si identifica soprattutto con le sue facciate barocche. Per questa ragione condivido la decisione del Parlamento tedesco di privilegiare la ricostruzione della stereometria e delle facciate barocche, e della cupola ottocentesca, rispetto a quella di tutti gli altri elementi.

Un'esauriente documentazione, frutto di un'accurata ricerca, ha consentito una ricostruzione fedele all'originale, e dunque a mio avviso autentica, sia degli elementi decisi dalla politica, sia di quelli aggiunti dal mio progetto.

that the façade has no civic or urban importance in itself, despite the fact that this building is identified in the collective memory above all with its Baroque façades. This is the reason why I agree with the German Parliament's decision to give priority to the reconstruction of the Baroque façades and the 19th-century dome over all other elements.

An extensive documentation, the result of careful research, has allowed for a reconstruction faithful to the original, and therefore in my opinion authentic, of both the elements decided by the politic and those added by my project.

Die Architektur des
Berliner Schlosses –
Humboldt Forums

L'architettura del
Berliner Schloss –
Humboldt Forum

The architecture of
Berliner Schloss –
Humboldt Forum

Luftbild der Stadtmitte, um 1930
Veduta aerea del Centro-Città, ca 1930
Aerial view of the city centre, about 1930

Die Identität des historischen Zentrums Berlins

Das im Zweiten Weltkrieg schwer beschädigte Berliner Schloss wurde 1950 von den politischen Machthabern der DDR dem Erdboden gleichgemacht, weil es als Symbol des preußischen Militarismus galt, vielleicht aber vor allem, weil das große Areal im Zentrum der Stadt der ideale Ort für politische Demonstrationen und Militärparaden war: eine Art Roter Platz Berlins.

In den fünf Jahrhunderten seiner Existenz war es das wichtigste Gebäude Berlins, sowohl in politisch-sozialer Hinsicht als auch in urbanarchitektonischer Hinsicht: Die wichtigsten Straßen, Plätze und Bauten des seit dem 18. Jahrhundert gewachsenen Stadtzentrums waren auf das Schloss bezogen.

Die Bauteile waren zahlreich und vielfältig: Dazu gehörten die Abschnitte der im Laufe von zweieinhalb Jahrhunderten gewachsenen Kurfürstenresidenz der Spätgotik und Renaissance; die Partien der von 1699

L'identità del Centro storico di Berlino

Il Castello di Berlino, gravemente danneggiato durante la Seconda Guerra mondiale, venne raso al suolo nel 1950 dai detentori del potere politico della RDT, perché ritenuto l'edificio simbolo del militarismo prussiano, ma forse soprattutto perché la vasta area centrale che esso occupava era il luogo ideale per le dimostrazioni politiche e le parate militari, per una sorta di Piazza Rossa di Berlino.

Nel corso dei cinque secoli della sua esistenza è stato l'edificio più importante di Berlino, sia dal punto di vista politico-sociale, sia dal punto di vista architettonico-urbano: le principali strade, piazze e palazzi del Centro Città, sviluppatosi a partire dal 18° secolo, si erano riferite al Castello.

Numerose e diverse erano le sue parti: quelle tardogotiche e rinascimentali della residenza dei principi brandeburghesi, costruite nel corso di due secoli e mezzo; quelle barocche, della residenza dei re prussiani,

The Identity of the Berlin Historical Centre

Berlin Palace, severely damaged during the Second World War, was razed in 1950 by the GDR's political power holders, because it was considered to be the symbolic building of Prussian militarism, but perhaps above all because the vast central area it occupied was the ideal place for political demonstrations and military parades, for a sort of Berlin Red Square.

During the five centuries of its existence, it was the most important building in Berlin: both from the social-political and the architectural-urban point of view – since the main streets, squares and palaces of the City Centre, which developed since 18th century, referred to the Berlin Palace.

Its parts were numerous and diverse: the late Gothic and Renaissance residence of the Brandenburg princes, built over two and a half centuries; the Baroque residence of the Prussian kings, built from 1699

Luftbild der Museumsinsel, um 1930

Veduta aerea dell'Isola dei Musei, ca 1930

Aerial view of Museum Island, about 1930

bis 1716 gebauten barocken königlichen Residenz von Andreas Schlüter, deren zweiter Teil von Eosander von Göthe; sowie die um die Mitte des 19. Jahrhunderts von Friedrich August Stüler errichtete Kuppel.

Um die alten Bauteile an das neue Gebäude anzupassen, unterbreiteten die beiden Architekten unterschiedliche Vorschläge. Schlüter forderte eine Umgestaltung sämtlicher Seiten des vorhandenen Gebäudes, während Eosander sich darauf beschränkte, lediglich den Abriss des Apothekenflügels zu fordern, der aus der Flucht der Barockfassade zum Lustgarten hervorragte.

Das Scheitern dieser Vorschläge erklärt die Abweichung einiger Elemente des Schlosses von dem Ideal der Symmetrie: Dies betrifft die nichtsymmetrische Anordnung der zwei Portale in der Fassade auf der Nord- und Südseite, den Vorsprung des abschließenden westlichen Trakts der Lustgartenfassade, das Rundtürmchen (Rondell) lediglich an der Südostecke und die leichte

costruita dal 1699 al 1716 - la prima parte sulla base del progetto di Andreas Schlüter e la seconda di Eosander von Göthe - e la cupola, costruita a metà Ottocento su progetto di Friedrich August Stüler.

Per accordare le parti preesistenti al nuovo edificio, gli architetti proposero diversi rimedi. Schlüter auspicò la trasformazione di tutti i lati dell'edificio esistente, mentre Eosander si limitò a proporre la demolizione del corpo di fabbrica della farmacia, l'Apothekerflügel, sporgente dal filo della facciata barocca rivolta verso il Lustgarten.

Il fallimento di tali proposte spiega lo scostamento di alcuni elementi del Castello dall'ideale della simmetria: la disposizione non-simmetrica dei due portali nella facciata dei lati nord e sud, l'avanzamento del solo tratto conclusivo ovest della facciata sul Lustgarten, la torretta circolare (Rondell) solo nell'angolo sud-est; la non esatta ortogonalità dei fronti maggiori e minori. La ricostruzione ha conservato tutte queste 'imperfezioni'.

to 1716 - the first part of it based on a design by Andreas Schlüter and the second part by Eosander von Göthe - and the dome, built in the mid-19th century according to a design by Friedrich August Stüler.

To harmonize the existing parts to the new building, the architects proposed various remedies. Schlüter advocated the transformation of all sides of the existing building, Eosander would have been content to demolish the pharmacy building, the Apothekerflügel (pharmacy wing), which protruded from the line of the Baroque façade facing the Lustgarten.

The failure of these proposals explains the deviation of some elements of the Palace from the ideal of symmetry: the asymmetrical disposition of the two portals in the façade on the north and south sides, the advancement of only the final western section of the façade towards the Lustgarten, the round tower (Rondell) only in the south-east corner; the not exact orthogonality of the major and minor sides. The recon-

Ansicht des Lustgartens mit Schlossbrücke,
Altem Museum, Dom und Schloss,
gezeichnet von Karl Friedrich Schinkel, 1823

Veduta del Lustgarten con lo Schlossbrücke,
l'Altes Museum, il Duomo e il Castello,
disegnata da Karl Friedrich Schinkel, 1823

View of Lustgarten with Schlossbrücke, Altes
Museum, Cathedral and Schloss, drawn by Karl
Friedrich Schinkel, 1823

Abweichung der Fassadenachsen vom 90-Grad-Winkel. Die Rekonstruktion hat all diese ›Unvollkommenheiten‹ bewahrt.

Große Architekten späterer Epochen erkannten den besonderen künstlerischen Wert der Architektur des Berliner Schlosses. Karl Friedrich Schinkel schrieb zu Beginn des 19. Jahrhunderts: »Das Schloß wird allgemein angesehen als ein Denkmal […], welches in seiner Würde und Pracht […] den ersten Gebäuden Europens in jeder Hinsicht gleichgestellt werden kann. […] Von eigentlich classischen Gebäuden, die in ihrer ganzen Idee etwas wirklich eigenthümliches und vorzüglich großartiges haben, besitzt Berlin nur zwei: das Königliche Schloß und das Zeughaus. Den Kunstwerth beider verdanken wir Schlüter […].«[5]

Um die Eigenständigkeit gegenüber den früheren Bauteilen des Schlosses zu betonen, schlug Schinkel vor, den vorspringenden Baukörper des Apothekenflügels hinter einer Baumwand zu verstecken: ein Vorschlag eines minimalen Ein-

Grandi architetti di epoche successive hanno riconosciuto lo specifico valore architettonico-artistico della parte barocca del Castello di Berlino. Ad esempio Karl Friedrich Schinkel all'inizio del 19° secolo: «Il Castello è generalmente ritenuto come un monumento […] che per dignità e decoro può stare alla pari con i primi edifici d'Europa. […] Di edifici veramente classici, nella cui concezione c'è qualcosa di autenticamente grande e singolare, Berlino ne ha solo due: il Castello reale e l'Arsenale. Il valore artistico dell'architettura di entrambi lo dobbiamo a Schlüter.»[5]

E, per rimarcarne l'autonomia rispetto alle fabbriche preesistenti, suggerì di nascondere il corpo della farmacia con una Baumwand (parete di alberi): una proposta minimale ma di successo, visto che un gruppo di alberi davanti alla farmacia esisteva ancora quando il Castello fu distrutto.

Circa un secolo dopo, anche l'elogio di Schlüter pronunciato da Adolf Loos, si riferisce in particolare

struction has preserved all these 'imperfections'.

Great architects of later epochs recognised the specific architectural and artistic value of the Baroque part of the Berlin Palace. For example, Karl Friedrich Schinkel, in the early 19th century: "The Berlin Palace is generally considered to be a monument which, in terms of dignity and decorum, can stand on a par with the first buildings in Europe. […] Berlin has only two truly classical buildings, in whose design there is something authentically grand and singular: the Royal Palace and the Arsenal. We owe the artistic value of the architecture of both to Schlüter."[5]

And to emphasise its autonomy from the existing buildings, he suggested hiding the pharmacy wing with a Baumwand (wall of trees): a minimal but successful proposal, given that a group of trees still existed when the Palace was destroyed.

Even Adolf Loos at the beginning of the 20th century praised the architect of the Baroque palace: "But every time architecture moves away

Der Boulevard Unter den Linden vom
Brandenburger Tor bis zum Berliner Schloss.
Foto um 1930

Il Boulevard Unter den Linden dalla Porta di
Brandeburgo al Castello. Foto ca 1930

The Boulevard Unter den Linden from the
Brandenburg Gate to the Berlin Palace.
Photo about 1930

griffs, der aber seinen Zweck erfüllte. Eine Baumgruppe stand noch vor der Apotheke, als das Schloss zerstört wurde.

Auch Adolf Loos' Würdigung Schlüters zu Beginn des folgenden Jahrhunderts bezieht sich auf das Barockschloss: »Aber jedesmal wenn sich die baukunst immer und immer wieder durch die kleinen, durch die ornamentiker, von ihrem großen vorbilde entfernt, ist der große baukünstler nahe, der sie wieder zur antike zurückführt. Fischer von Erlach im süden, Schlüter im norden waren mit recht die großen meister des achtzehnten jahrhunderts. Und an der schwelle des neunzehnten stand Schinkel. Wir haben ihn vergessen. Möge das licht dieser überragenden gestalt auf unsere kommende baukünstlergeneration fallen!«[6]

Von der früher als das Schloss entstandenen mittelalterlichen Altstadt, die durch Krieg und die DDR zerstört wurde, ist fast nichts mehr übrig geblieben. Hingegen ist das westlich gelegene monumentale Stadtzentrum

al Castello barocco: «Ma ogni volta che l'architettura si allontana dal suo modello con i minori, i decorativisti, ricompare il grande architetto che la riconduce all'antichità. Fischer von Erlach nel Sud, Schlüter nel Nord furono a buon diritto i grandi maestri del secolo diciottesimo. E sulla soglia del diciannovesimo secolo c'era Schinkel. Lo abbiamo dimenticato. Possa questa straordinaria architettura illuminare l'arte degli architetti della prossima generazione!»[6]

Quasi nulla è rimasto della città medioevale (Altstadt), nata prima del Castello, distrutta dalla guerra e poi dalla politica della RDT; mentre il Centro storico monumentale, costruito nel Sette-Ottocento in riferimento al Castello e ampiamente ricostruito nel dopoguerra già al tempo della RDT, è quasi tutto ancora esistente.

Sul tracciato del «sentiero dei cavalieri», che portava sovrani e aristocratici a caccia nel Tiergarten, si sviluppò nel corso del 18° secolo il gran boulevard Unter den Linden,

from its model with the lesser, decorativists, the great architect reappears who takes it back to antiquity. Fischer von Erlach in the South, Schlüter in the North were rightly the great masters of the eighteenth century. And on the threshold of the 19th century there was Schinkel. May this extraordinary architecture illuminate the art of the architects of the next generation!"[6]

Almost nothing remains of the medieval town (Altstadt), which was built before the Palace, destroyed by the war and then by the GDR's urban planning politics; almost everything remains of the monumental historic centre, built in the 18th and 19th centuries in reference to the Palace, and extensively rebuilt after the war, already from the time of the GDR.

The "knights' way", which led kings and aristocrats to hunt in the Tiergarten, has developed over the centuries into the grand boulevard Unter den Linden during the 18th century, an uninterrupted sequence of public and private palaces, built

Die Museumsinsel und das Schloss
aus der Vogelperspektive

Veduta a volo d'uccello dell'Isola dei Musei
e del Castello

Bird's eye view of Museum Island
and the Berlin Palace

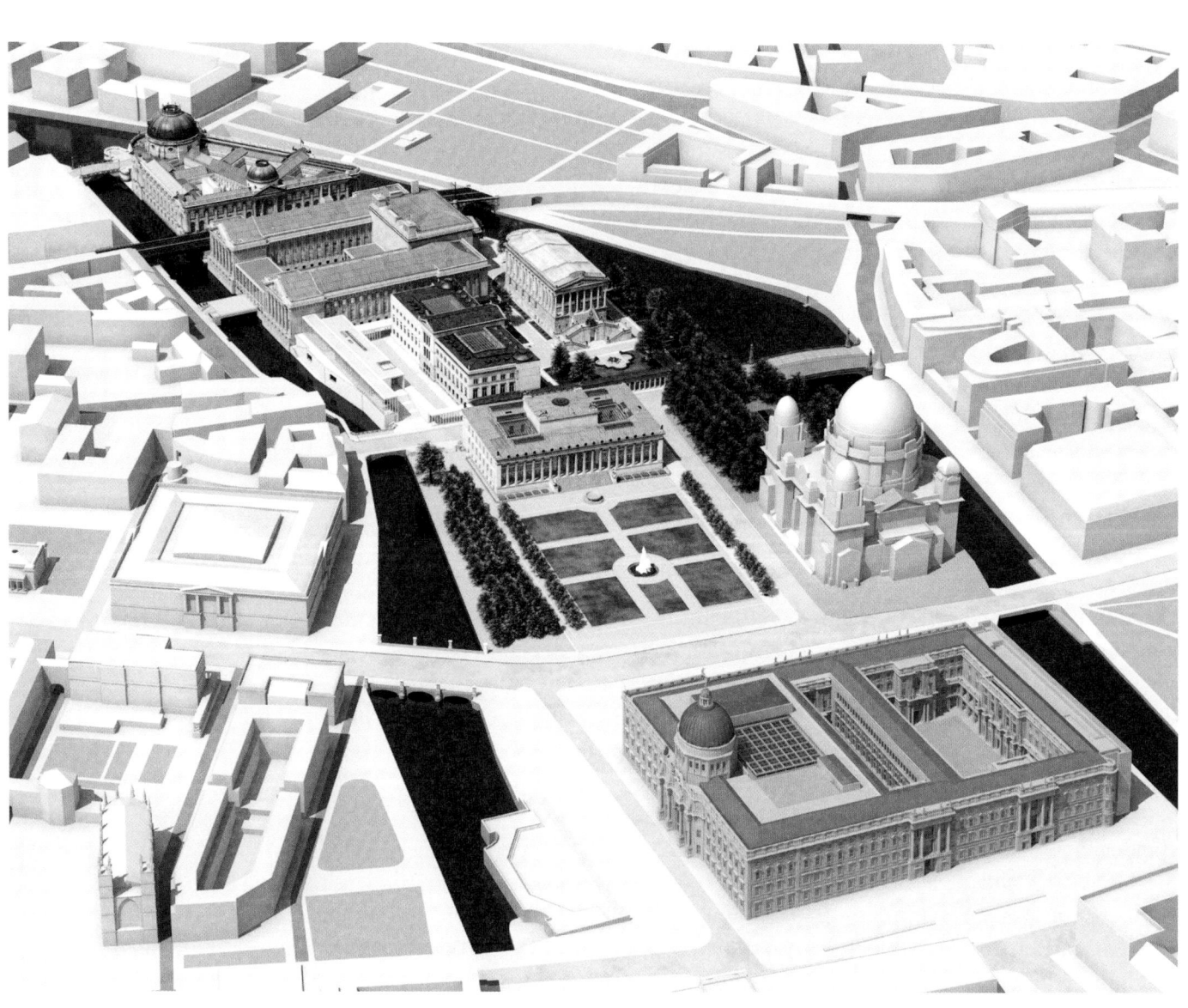

aus dem 18. und 19. Jahrhundert noch fast vollständig vorhanden, und wurde auf das Schloss in der Nachkriegszeit schon von der DDR weitgehend rekonstruiert.

Entlang dem ›Reitweg‹, auf dem Könige und Adelige sich zur Jagd in den Tiergarten begaben, entwickelte sich im 18. Jahrhundert der Prachtboulevard Unter den Linden, eine Abfolge öffentlicher und privater Paläste und Palais, die im königlichen Auftrag beziehungsweise unter königlicher Kontrolle errichtet wurden, bis hin zum Brandenburger Tor, das sich der König als Propyläen zum Schloss gedacht hatte und das sein Architekt Langhans entwarf.

Am Nordrand des Lustgartens entstand vor dem Schloss im 19. Jahrhundert nach dem Willen der preußischen Herrscher die Museumsinsel mit ihren fünf berühmten Museumspalästen.

Im vorderen Lustgarten wurden die Gebäude errichtet, die symbolisch für das Militär (Zeughaus), die Religion (Dom) und die Kultur (Altes Museum) stehen und zusammen mit

una sequenza ininterrotta di palazzi pubblici e privati, eretti per ordine o concessione dei sovrani, fino ad arrivare alla Porta Brandeburgo, pensata dal re e disegnata dal suo architetto Langhans, come i Propilei al Castello.

Nell'area a nord del suo Lustgarten (giardino di delizie) si è sviluppata nel corso dell'Ottocento, per volontà dei sovrani prussiani, la Museumsinsel (isola del Museo), con i suoi cinque famosi palazzi-museo.

Attorno al Lustgarten furono eretti gli edifici simbolo del potere militare (l'Arsenale), religioso (il Duomo), culturale (l'Altes Museum), conformando, assieme al Castello, una sorta di 'Piazza dei Quattro Poteri', in particolare il grandioso 'colonnato greco' dell'Altes Museum (allora Neues Museum) venne concepito da Schinkel come un'architettura degna di stare dirimpetto al Castello.

Con la scomparsa del Castello andò perduta anche la possibilità di comprendere il senso urbano e architettonico dei principali luoghi ed edifici del Centro-città. Un'impossi-

by order or concession of the kings, up to the Brandenburg Gate, conceived by the king and designed by his architect Langhans as the Propylaea to the Castle.

In the area to the north of the Lustgarten (garden of delight), the Museumsinsel (Island of Museum) with its five famous museum palaces was developed during the 19th century at the behest of the Prussian sovereigns.

Around the Lustgarten, the buildings symbolizing military power (the Arsenal), religious power (the Cathedral), and cultural power (the Altes Museum) were erected, forming, together with the Palace, a sort of 'Square of the Four Powers'; in particular the grandiose 'Greek colonnade' of the Altes Museum (then Neues Museum) was conceived by Schinkel as an architecture worthy of standing in front of the Berlin Palace.

With its disappearance, the possibility of understanding the urban and architectural sense of the main places and buildings in the city cen-

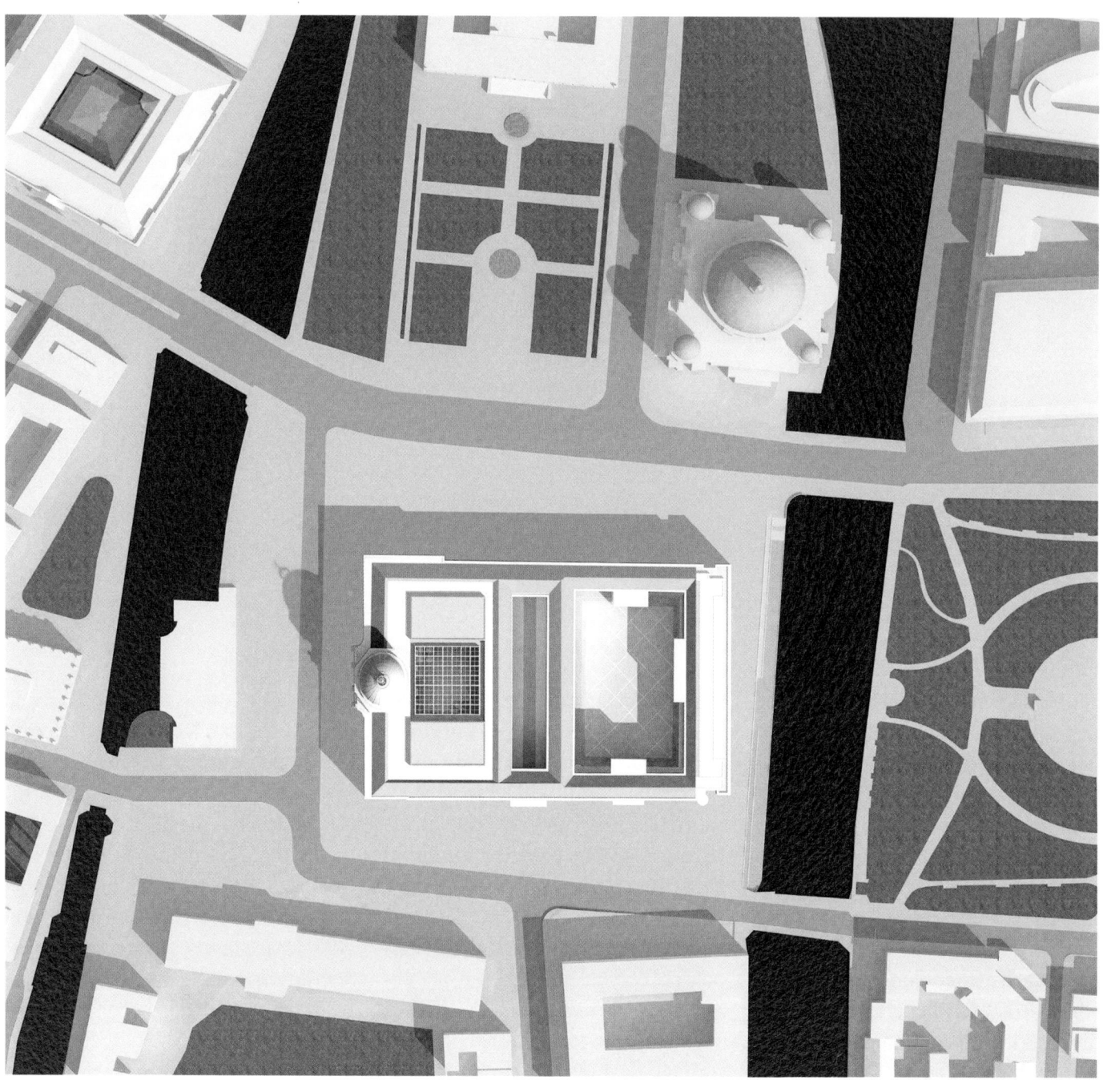

Planvolumetrie des neuen Berliner Schlosses

Planivolumetrico del nuovo Castello di Berlino

Planvolumetry of the new Berlin Palace

dem Schloss einen ›Platz der vier Mächte‹ bildeten; die großzügige ›griechische Kolonnade‹ des Alten Museums (damals Neues Museum) wurde von Schinkel als würdevolle, frontal zum Schloss ausgerichtete Architektur konzipiert.

Mit dem Verschwinden des Schlosses verlor sich auch die urbane und architektonische Bedeutung der wichtigsten Plätze und Gebäude im Stadtzentrum. Dieses Manko wurde durch die folgenden Nutzungen des Ortes bekräftigt. Dazu zählt auch die Errichtung des Palastes der Republik (1973 bis 1976), der rund fünfzehn Jahren später, nach dem Ende der DDR, geschlossen und schließlich nach etwa ebenso vielen Jahren abgerissen wurde.

Mit der Rekonstruktion des Schlosses wird der räumliche Maßstab der umliegenden Plätze wiedergewonnen. Allgemein kann man sagen: Das Schloss kehrt als *Lehrer der Stadtgeschichte* in die Stadt zurück, deren *Regisseur* es war.

bilità confermata dalle successive trasformazioni e usi dell'area: fra queste quella del Palazzo della Repubblica, qui costruito dal 1973 al 1976, dismesso circa quindici anni dopo in corrispondenza con la caduta della RDT, e, dopo altrettanti anni, distrutto.

Con il ritorno del Castello, le piazze che lo circondano riacquistano la loro originaria misura spaziale. In generale si può dire che il Castello ritorna come *maestro di storia urbana* nella città di cui è stato *regista*.

tre was also lost. An impossibility confirmed by the successive transformations and uses of the area: among these that of Palace of the Republic, built here from 1973 to 1976, closed about fifteen years later to coincide with the fall of the GDR, and, after about as many years, destroyed.

With the reconstruction of the Berlin Palace, the surrounding squares regained their original spatial dimensions. In general, it can be said that the Berlin Palace returns as *teacher of urban history* in the city of which it was the *director*.

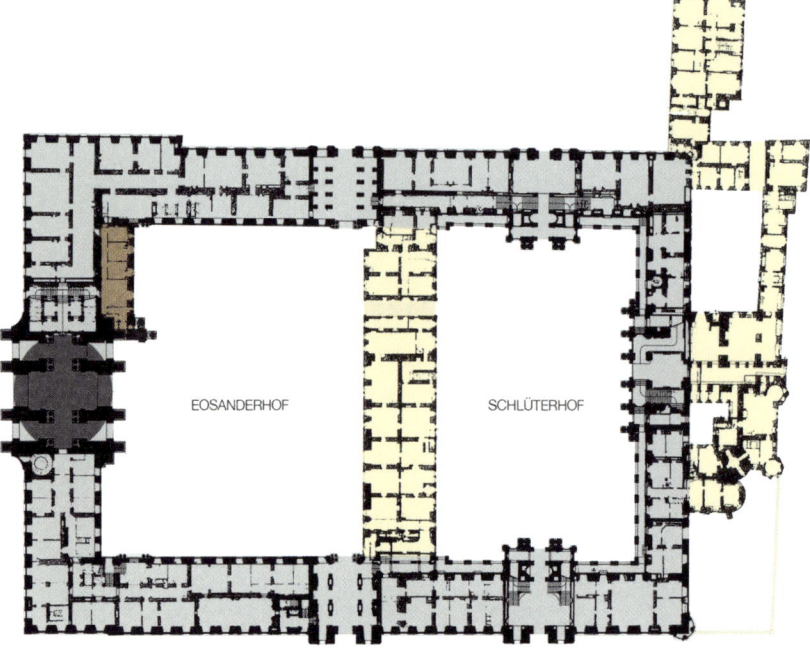

DAS BERLINER SCHLOSS VOR DER ZERSTÖRUNG
IL CASTELLO DI BERLINO PRIMA DELLA DISTRUZIONE
THE BERLIN PALACE BEFORE DESTRUCTION

- Vorbarocke Bauten   Costruzioni prebarocche   Pre-baroque buildings
- Barocke Bauten   Costruzioni barocche   Baroque buildings
- Kuppel   Cupola   Dome
- Spätere Anbau   Aggiunta successiva   Later addition

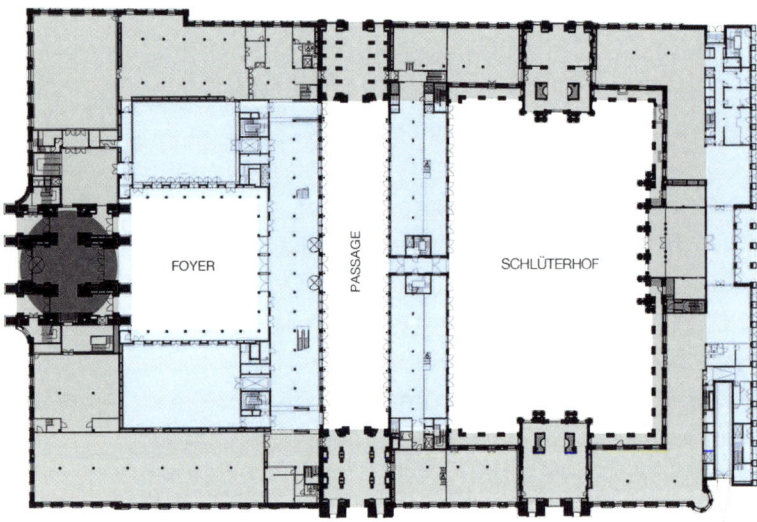

DAS NEUE BERLINER SCHLOSS - HUMBOLDT FORUM (2012-2021)
IL NUOVO CASTELLO DI BERLINO - HUMBOLDT FORUM (2012-2021)
THE NEW BERLIN PALACE - HUMBOLDT FORUM (2012-2021)

- Rekonstruierte Bauteile   Corpi di fabbrica ricostruiti   Reconstructed building elements
- Neue Bauteile   Nuovi corpi di fabbrica   New building elements
- Rekonstruierte Kuppel   Cupola ricostruita   Reconstructed dome

Planimetrischer Vergleich zwischen dem alten und dem neuen Schloss

Confronto planimetrico fra il vecchio e il nuovo Castello

Planimetric comparison between the old and the new Berlin Palace

Eine Kombination von rekonstruiertem Alten und modernem Neuen

Das neue Berliner Schloss – Humboldt Forum ist ein den Brüdern Humboldt gewidmetes Zentrum für Kunst und Kultur, ein »Ort der Begegnung mit Weltkulturen« – vor allem den außereuropäischen. Es ist ein einheitliches Bauwerk, barock und modern: ein Ganzes aus unterschiedlichen, in sich architektonisch vollendeten Orten, die aus einer einzigartigen Kombination von *rekonstruiertem Alten* und *modernem Neuen* bestehen, die einander ergänzen.

Das *rekonstruierte Alte* wird repräsentiert durch die vom Deutschen Bundestag vorgeschriebenen, schon erwähnten Teile sowie durch die in meinem Entwurf hinzugefügten Elemente: die Durchgänge und die Fassaden der drei Portale zum westlichen Hof (Eosanderhof) sowie die Verkleidung und Ergänzung der Kuppel mit Laterne und Kreuz.

Das *moderne Neue* besteht aus fünf Baukörpern: außen der Bauteil

Una combinazione di Antico ricostruito e moderno Nuovo

Il nuovo Castello di Berlino (Berliner Schloss – Humboldt Forum) è un Centro d'Arte e Cultura – il «luogo dell'incontro con le culture del mondo», soprattutto extraeuropee – dedicato ai fratelli Humboldt. E' un edificio unitario, barocco e moderno: una composizione di luoghi architettonicamente compiuti, risultanti da una singolare combinazione di *Antico ricostruito* e *moderno Nuovo*, che si completano l'uno con l'altro.

L'*Antico ricostruito* è rappresentato, oltreché dai già menzionati elementi decisi dal Parlamento tedesco, da quelli aggiunti dal mio progetto: gli atri e le facciate dei tre portali in origine rivolte verso la corte occidentale (Eosanderhof), il rivestimento, e il completamento con lanterna e croce, della cupola.

Il *moderno Nuovo* consiste in cinque nuovi corpi di fabbrica: uno solo all'esterno, nell'area delle fabbriche

A combination of reconstructed Old and modern New

The new Berlin Palace (Berliner Schloss – Humboldt Forum) is a Centre for Art and Culture – the "meeting place for world cultures", especially non-European ones – dedicated to the Humboldt brothers. It is an unified building, baroque and modern: a composition of architectural accomplished places, characterised by a singular combination of *reconstructed Old* and *modern New*, complementing each other.

In addition to the already mentioned elements prescribed by the German Parliament, the *reconstructed Old* is represented by those added by my project, namely the atria and the façades of the three portals originally facing the western court (Eosanderhof), the covering, and completion with lantern and cross, of the dome.

The *modern New* consists of five new buildings: one outside, in the area of the Renaissance buildings

Vergleich der Proportionen zwischen der rekonstruierten Nordfassade und der neuen Fassade zur Spree

Comparazione delle proporzioni della ricostruita facciata nord con la nuova facciata sulla Sprea

Comparison of proportions of the reconstructed north façade with the new façade on the Spree

anstelle der ehemaligen Renaissancebauten des Spreeflügels, im Inneren die vier Bauteile im Bereich des einst barocken Eosanderhofs.

Mit Ausnahme des *Stils* sehen das Alte und das Neue aus wie Bestandteile desselben Gebäudes – des idealen Gebäudes, welches das realisierte anstrebte – sodass es nicht mehr sinnvoll ist, von einem *Vorher* und einem *Nachher* zu sprechen. Der Eindruck, dass alle Baukörper – egal ob original oder rekonstruiert – zusammen entstanden seien, führt den über die Geschichte des Ortes nicht informierten Besucher zur Frage, warum einige eine moderne und nicht eine barocke Fassade haben.

Man kann hier von einer ungewöhnlichen Rekonstruktion sprechen. Üblicherweise – man denke an die Alte Pinakothek in München oder an das Neue Museum in Berlin – ist das Alte das Original, das die Zerstörung überstanden hat und mehr oder weniger restauriert werden konnte, während das Neue das Rekonstruierte ist, dessen Formensprache von seiner ursprünglichen

rinascimentali affacciate sulla Sprea, gli altri quattro all'interno, nell'area dell'ex corte barocca Eosanderhof.

A meno dello *stile*, sembra quasi che l'Antico e il Nuovo siano fin dall'origine parti integranti di uno stesso edificio – l'edificio ideale a cui tendeva quello realmente esistito – per cui non ha senso parlare di un *prima* e un *dopo*. La sensazione che tutti i corpi di fabbrica, non importa se originali o ricostruiti, siano sempre stati assieme, porta il visitatore non informato sulla storia del luogo a chiedere perché mai alcuni di essi abbiano una facciata moderna anziché barocca.

Si può parlare di una ricostruzione inusuale, perché solitamente – si pensi ad esempi all'Alte Pinakothek di Monaco o al Neues Museum di Berlino – l'Antico è l'Originale sopravvissuto alla distruzione e più o meno restaurato, mentre il Nuovo è il Ricostruito, il cui linguaggio vuol comunicare sia la sua originaria appartenenza all'edificio sia la cesura nella sua storia.

facing the Spree, the other four in the area of the Eosanderhof.

Except for the *style*, it almost seems as if the Old and the New are from the beginning integral parts of the same building – the ideal building to which the one that actually existed tended – so that it no longer makes sense to speak of a *before* and an *after*. The feeling that all parts of the building, no matter whether original or reconstructed, have always been together leads the visitor uninformed about the history of the place to ask why some of them have a modern rather than Baroque façade.

We can speak of a unusual reconstruction, because normaly – think for example of the Alte Pinakothek in Munich or the Neues Museum in Berlin – the Old is the Original that survived destruction and was more or less restored, while the New is the Reconstructed, whose language is intended to communicate both its original belonging to the building and the caesura in its history.

Unlike such examples, in the case of the Berliner Schloss the Old

Vergleich der Proportionen zwischen
der rekonstruierten Fassade und
der neuen Fassade des Schlüterhofs

Comparazione delle proporzioni della
facciata ricostruita con la nuova facciata
dello Schlüterhof

Comparison of proportions of the
reconstructed façade with the
new façade of the Schlüterhof

Zugehörigkeit zum Gebäude, aber auch von der Zäsur in dessen Geschichte erzählen will.

Anders als bei diesen Beispielen gibt es im Fall des Berliner Schlosses das Alte und Neue nicht in derselben Fassade nebeneinander, denn das rekonstruierte Alte ist hier nicht der zufällig erhalten gebliebene Teil eines zerstörten Gebäudes, sondern ein von einem Entwurf für das ganze Gebäude bestimmter Teil. Das Zusammenspiel von Alt und Neu folgt der Absicht, die architektonisch-städtebaulichen Potenziale des alten Schlosses wiederzugewinnen und weiterzuentwickeln.

Dafür wurden das Gebäude insgesamt als Palast, die Innenhöfe als öffentliche Plätze - Piazza (der *Schlüterhof*), Forum (die *Passage*) und Theater (das *Foyer*) -, die Portale als Stadttore und die Fassaden als Kombination von Mauern und Säulen konzipiert.

Diversamente da tali esempi, nel caso del Berliner Schloss l'Antico e il Nuovo non si trovano mai l'uno accanto all'altro nella stessa facciata, perché l'Antico ricostruito non è la parte casualmente sopravvissuta a una distruzione, ma una parte decisa da un progetto per l'intero edificio.

Il gioco di Antico e Moderno è guidato dall'intenzione di riacquistare e sviluppare le potenzialità architettonico-urbane dell'antico Castello.

A tal fine l'edificio nel suo insieme è stato concepito come un Palazzo, i cortili interni come luoghi pubblici - rispettivamente Piazza (lo *Schlüterhof*), Foro (il *Passage*), e Teatro (il *Foyer*) -, i portali di ingresso come Porta di città e le facciate come combinazione di Muri e Colonne.

and the New are never found next to each other in the same façade, because the Old was not accidentally decided by an unwanted destruction, but wanted by a project of the whole building.

The relationship between Old and Modern is directet by the purpose to regain and develop the architectural-urban potential of the lost baroque building.

For this intent, the building has been conceived as a Palace, the inner courtyards as public Places - respectively Piazza (the *Schlüterhof*), Forum (the *Passage*), Theatre (the *Foyer*) -, the entrance portals as City Gates, the façades as a combination of Walls and Columns.

Berliner Schloss nach dem vermutlich ersten Entwurf für die Neugestaltung nach Plänen von Andreas Schlüter, Kupferstich von Peter Schenk, 1702

Il presunto primo progetto di trasformazione del Castello di Berlino, concepito da Andreas Schlüter, incisione su rame di Peter Schenk, 1702

The presumed first transformation project of Berlin Palace, conceived by Andreas Schlüter, engraving by Peter Schenk, 1702

Das Gebäude als vierflügeliger Palast

Um den alten Palast, die Residenz der brandenburgischen Kurfürsten, in das repräsentative Schloss der preußischen Könige zu verwandeln, schlug der Architekt Andreas Schlüter an der Schwelle des 18. Jahrhunderts ein ›vierflügeliges‹ Gebäude nach dem Vorbild italienischer Renaissance- und Barockpaläste vor. Dafür war auch eine Um- und Neugestaltung der heterogenen Bebauung des Spreeflügels geplant.

An der Stelle des von Schlüter entworfenen, aber nicht realisierten Spreeflügels befindet sich heute der neue Baukörper, der sich mit den drei rekonstruierten barocken Flügeln so verbindet, dass ein Palast mit rechteckigem Grundriss von 180 x 120 Metern und einer Höhe von 30 Metern entsteht, dazu eine Kuppel, die sich bis zu 70 Meter über dem Westportal erhebt.

Seine Formensprache lässt sich besser als durch eine abstrakt-stilistische Einordnung mit der architek-

L'edificio come Palazzo a quattro ali

Per trasformare il vecchio Castello-residenza dei principi brandeburghesi nel prestigioso palazzo dei re prussiani, alle soglie del 18° secolo l'architetto Andreas Schlüter concepì un edificio 'a quattro ali', sull'esempio dei palazzi italiani del Rinascimento e del Barocco. Aveva perciò previsto anche una profonda e estesa trasformazione dell'eterogenea edificazione affacciata sulla Sprea.

Nei contorni della Spreeflügel (ala verso il fiume Sprea) immaginata e non realizzata da Schlüter, si trova ora un nuovo corpo di fabbrica che si unisce a quelli ricostruiti generando un palazzo con una pianta rettangolare di circa 180 x 120 metri e un'altezza di 30, con una cupola che si eleva sopra il portale occidentale fino a 70 metri.

Il suo linguaggio si spiega, piuttosto che con un' astratta classificazione stilistica, con il compito architettonico-urbano di portare a com-

The building as a Palace with four wings

In order to transform the old residence of the Brandenburg princes into the prestigious palace of the Prussian kings, at the turn of the 18th century architect Andreas Schlüter conceived a 'four-wing' building, architecturally unified on the example of Italian Renaissance and Baroque palaces. He therefore also envisaged extensive transformation of the heterogeneous building overlooking the Spree.

In the contours of the Spreeflügel (wing toward the Spree river) imagined and not realised by Schlüter, there is now a new building, which joins the reconstructed Baroque ones, generating a palace with a rectangular ground plan of approximately 180 x 120 metres and a height of 30, with a dome rising above the western portal up to 70 metres.

Its language is also explained – rather than an abstract stylistic classification – by the architectur-

Luftbild des alten Berliner Schlosses, um 1930
Veduta aerea del vecchio Castello di Berlino, ca 1930
Aerial view of the old Berlin Palace, about 1930

tonisch-städtebaulichen Aufgabe erklären: Seine Aufgabe besteht darin, die ursprüngliche Idee des vierflügeligen Palasts zu vervollständigen.

Die zeitlos-modern anmutende Architektur der Fassade an der Spree steht im Dialog mit den drei rekonstruierten Fassaden: durch eine vertikale Gliederung in drei fast gleich hohe und sich gleichende Geschosse und einem Attikageschoss, einen gleichen Abstand zwischen den Fensterachsen sowie durch die Größe der hundert Öffnungen – sechs Meter hoch, drei Meter breit, 1,30 Meter tief –, die damit den barocken Portalen vergleichbar werden. Dadurch präsentiert sich die gelochte Fensterwand als eine Sequenz aus Trilithen beziehungsweise als Loggienfassade, die auf den öffentlichen Charakter des Gebäudes hinweist.

Diese Fassade mag denen schmucklos erscheinen, die das ›Ornament‹ als etwas begreifen, das zur Malerei oder Skulptur, aber nicht zum Wesentlichen der Architektur gehört. Doch wird das Verhältnis zwischen tragenden und lastenden

pimento l'originaria idea del palazzo a quattro ali.

L'architettura della facciata sulla Sprea, che trasmette la sensazione di una modernità senza tempo, si accorda a quella delle tre facciate ricostruite, riproponendone l'articolazione verticale in tre piani quasi uguali e in un piano attico, la distanza fra gli assi delle finestre, la dimensione delle sue cento aperture – mediamente alte sei metri, larghe tre e profonde un metro e trenta – comparabile con quella dei portali barocchi. Talché la parete finestrata si presenta come una sequenza di triliti, una facciata di logge che suggerisce il carattere pubblico dell'edificio.

Questa facciata può apparire disadorna a chi intenda l'"ornamento" come qualcosa che attiene alla pittura o alla scultura, ma non all'essenza dell'architettura: trascurando ad esempio il fatto che la proporzione fra gli elementi portanti e portati è qui suggerita dall'umana percezione della stabilità piuttosto che dalla tecnica delle costruzioni. In questo senso il razionalismo di que-

al-urban purpose of realising the original idea of the four-winged building.

The architecture of the façade on the Spree, which transmits the feeling of timeless modernity, accords with that of the three reconstructed façades, reproposing its vertical articulation in three almost equal storeys and in a attic one, the distance between the axes of the windows, the size of its one hundred openings – on average six metres high, three metres wide and one meter and thirty centimetres deep – comparable to that of Baroque portals. So that the windowed wall presents itself as a sequence of triliths, as a façade of loggias, suggesting the public character of the building.

This façade may appear unadorned to those who understand 'ornament' as something pertaining to painting or sculpture, but not to the essence of architecture: overlooking, for example, the fact that the proportion between supporting and supported elements is here suggested by the human perception of

Luftbild des neuen Berliner Schlosses, 2022

Veduta aerea del nuovo Castello di Berlino, 2022

Aerial view of the old Berlin Palace, 2022

Elementen eher vom menschlichen Empfinden für Stabilität beeinflusst als von der Bautechnik. In diesem Sinne bedeutet der Rationalismus dieser Fassade keineswegs eine Reduktion der Architektur auf die Konstruktion. Der neue Spreeflügel steht nicht für sich, sondern ist nur im Kontext des rekonstruierten Barockpalastes des Berliner Schlosses zu verstehen.

Zum ersten Mal in der Geschichte dieses Ortes ist der östlichen Gebäudeseite heute ein öffentlicher Raum vorgelagert, eine *piazzetta* an der Spree, die über Rampen und szenografisch gestaltete Treppen mit dem Flussufer verbunden ist. In der Mitte der Fassade öffnet sich eine Eingangshalle, die seitlich von Cafés und Restaurants gesäumt wird.

sta facciata non significa affatto riduzione dell'architettura alla costruzione. La nuova Spreeflügel non è un edificio autonomo: la sua architettura si spiega solo nel contesto del ricostruito palazzo barocco del Castello di Berlino.

L'area libera antistante al fronte est dell'edificio, per la prima volta nella storia del luogo, è uno spazio pubblico, una *piazzetta* sulla Sprea, collegata da rampe e scalinate scenografiche con la riva del fiume. Nel tratto centrale della facciata si apre un portico d'ingresso, in quelli laterali si trovano caffè e ristoranti.

stability rather than by building technique. The new Spreeflügel is not a stand-alone building: its architecture can only be explained in the context of the reconstructed baroque building of the Berlin Palace.

The open area in front of the new east front of the building is, for the first time in the history of the site, a public space, a *piazzetta* on the Spree, connected by ramps and scenic stairs with the river bank. In the central section of the façade is an entrance portico, in the side ones are cafés and restaurants.

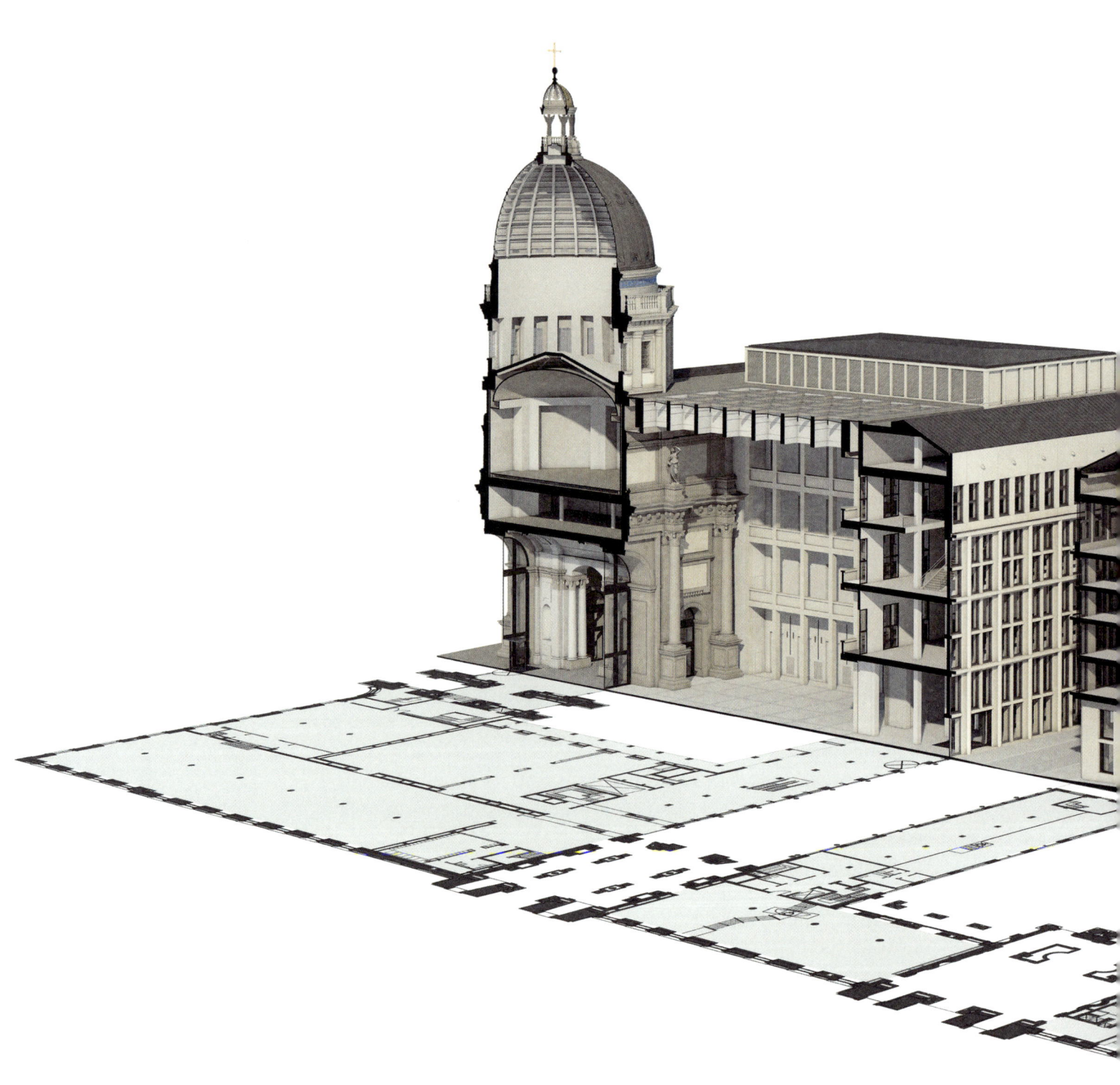

Schnittperspektive

Sezione prospettica

Section perspective

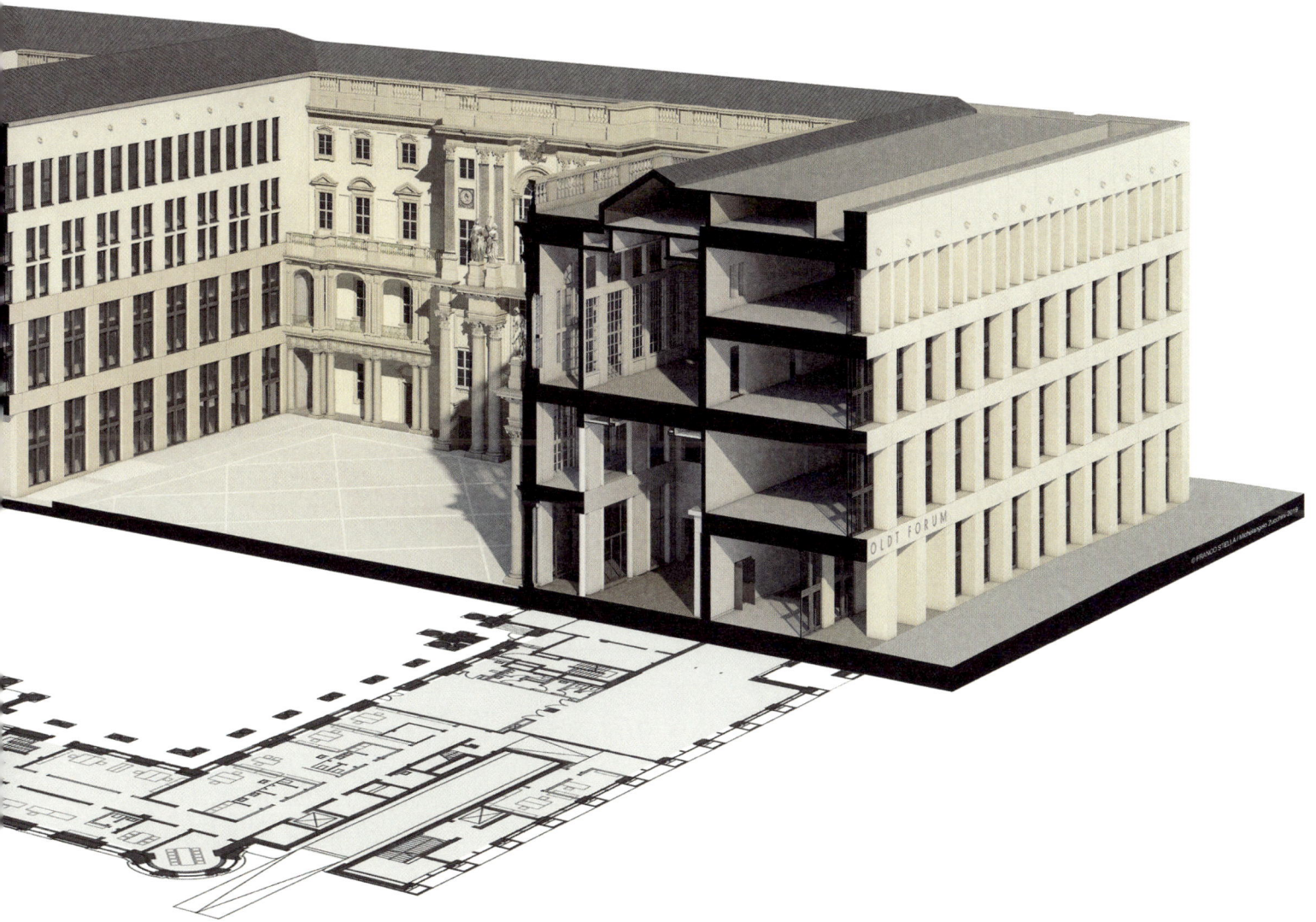

Ansichten

Prospetti

Elevations

| Die Architektur des Berliner Schlosses – Humboldt Forums | L'architettura del Berliner Schloss – Humboldt Forum | The architecture of Berliner Schloss – Humboldt Forum |

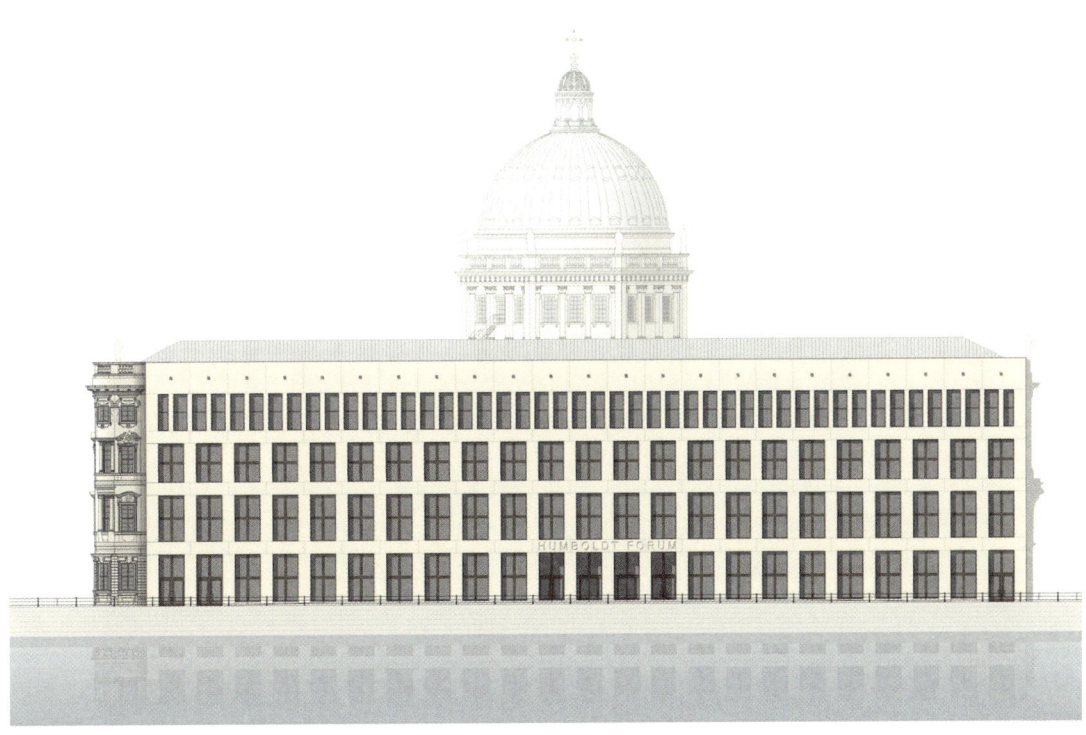

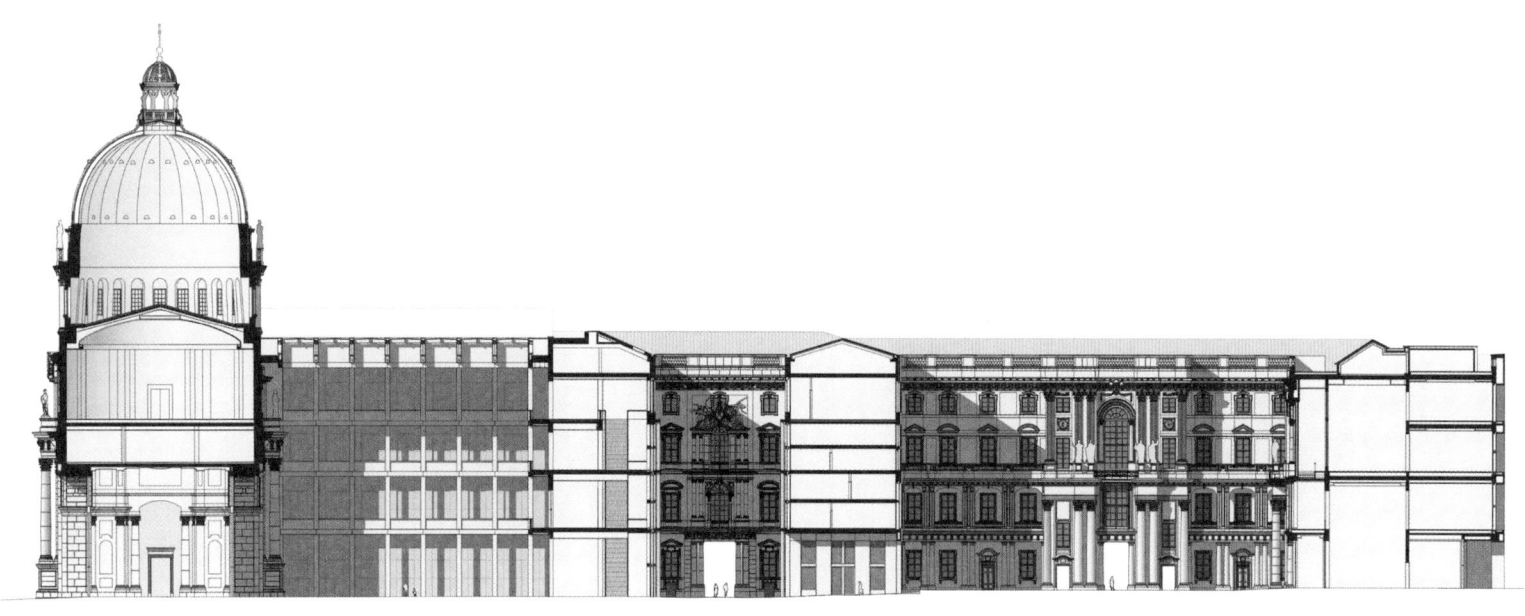

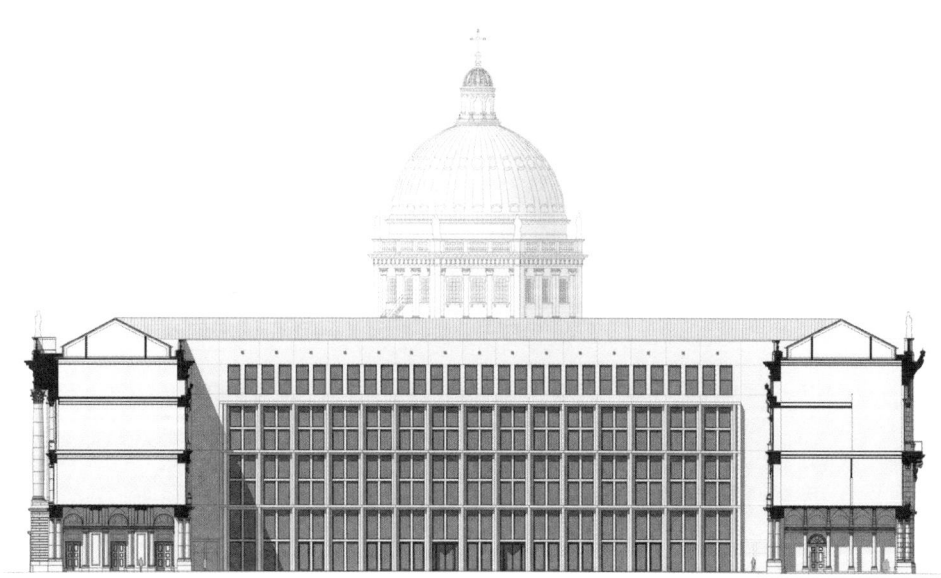

Schnittansichten

Prospetti-Sezioni

Elevations-Sections

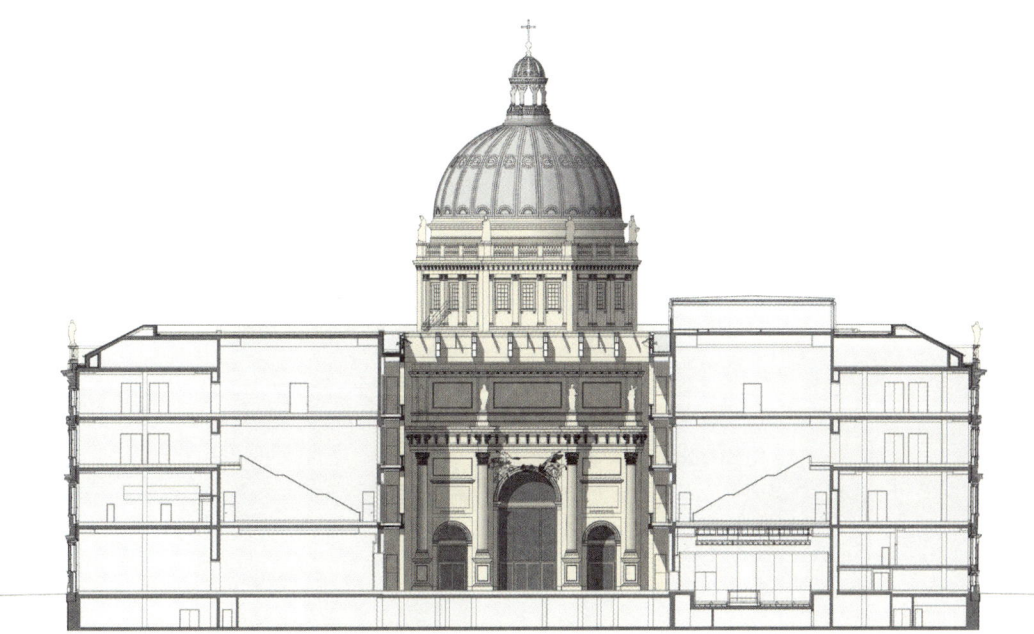

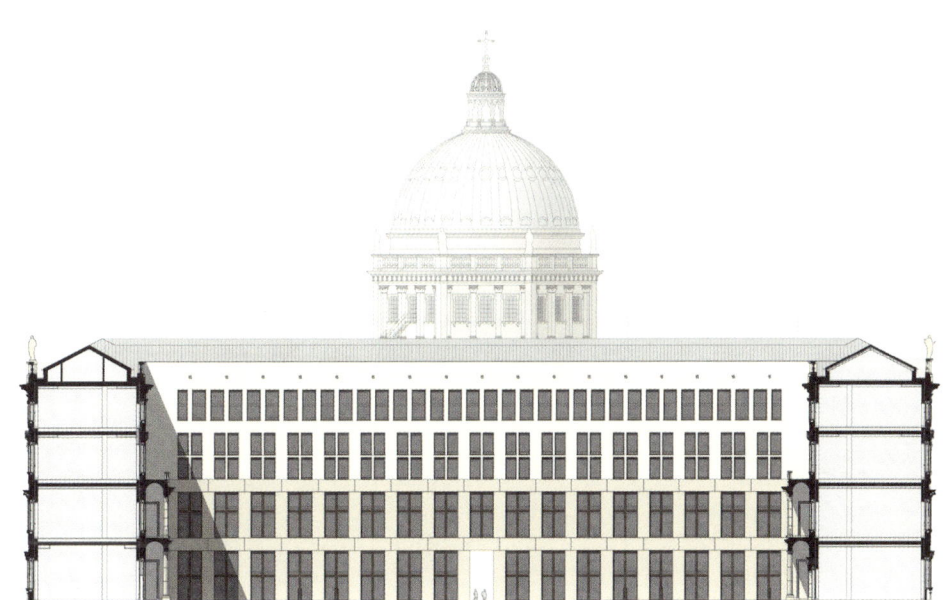

Portal V des Schlüterhofs mit Durchsicht nach Portal I:
Gemälde von Eduard Gaertner, um 1830

Portale V dello Schlüterhof con vista del Portale I:
dipinto di Eduard Gaertner, ca 1830

Portal V of the Schlüterhof with view of Portal I:
painting by Eduard Gaertner, about 1830

Die Portale als Stadttore

Die fünf Eingangsportale, mit Säulen, Lisenen und Figuren reich geschmückt, traten sowohl zur Stadt als auch zu den Höfen stark hervor. Entworfen in Anlehnung an antike Triumphbögen und Stadttore, waren sie die deutlichsten Zeichen der Bedeutung des Barockschlosses für die Stadt.

Sie führten in zwei Höfe: drei in den Eosanderhof und zwei in den Schlüterhof; weitere Portale führten dann von den Höfen zu den königlichen Wohnungen und den wichtigsten Repräsentationsräumen. Alle Portale wurden originalgetreu rekonstruiert und erhielten damit ihre Funktion als Stadttore zurück. Durch die hiermit erfolgte Verbindung der Stadtplätze mit den Gebäudehöfen entstehen drei durchgehende Achsen öffentlicher Räume – zwei in Nord-Süd- und eine quer durch das neue Berliner Schloss in West-Ost-Richtung.

I portali come Porte di città

I cinque portali d'ingresso, riccamente adorni di colonne, lesene e statue, risaltavano con forza nelle facciate, sia in quelle rivolte verso la città che verso le corti. Disegnati ad imitazione di antichi Archi trionfali e Porte di città, erano il segno più evidente del valore urbano del Castello barocco.

Introducevano a due cortili: tre allo Eosanderhof e due allo Schlüterhof; altri portali introducevano poi agli appartamenti reali e alle principali stanze di rappresentanza. Tutti i portali, fedelmente ricostruiti, hanno ritrovato la loro originaria funzione di Porta di città. Attraverso di essi lo spazio pubblico esterno si salda con quello interno lungo tre assi che attraversano tutto l'edificio, due in direzione nord-sud, e uno ovest-est.

The portals as City Gates

The five entrance portals had a strong prominence in the façades, both those facing the city and those facing the courtyards. Designed in imitation of ancient triumphal arches and city gates, they were the most evident sign of the Baroque Palace's urban value.

Richly decorated with columns, pilasters and statues, they led to two courtyards: three to the Eosanderhof and two to the Schlüterhof; other portals led to the royal appartments and the main representative rooms. All the portals, faithfully reconstructed, have regained their original function as city gates. Through them the external public space is joined with the internal one along three axes that cross the whole building, two in north-south direction and one west-east direction.

Der einstige Schlüterhof:
Gemälde von Eduard Gaertner, um 1830

Il precedente Schlüterhof:
Dipinto di Eduard Gaertner, intorno al 1830

The former Schlüterhof:
Painting by Eduard Gaertner, about 1830

Schlüterhof

Blick auf die rekonstruierten Ost- und Südfassaden
und die neue Westfassade

Veduta delle ricostruite facciate est e sud
e della nuova facciata ovest

View of the reconstructed east and south façades
and the new west façade

Die Höfe als öffentliche Plätze

Das alte Schloss hatte zwei öffentliche Plätze, das neue hat drei: den rekonstruierten und ergänzten *Schlüterhof*, die *Passage* und das überdachte *Foyer*. Die beiden neuen Höfe wurden im gemäß der Ausschreibung voll überbaubaren Bereich des Eosanderhofs gewonnen: Sie wurden so angelegt, dass sie auf seine drei Portale Bezug nehmen und dadurch mit den umliegenden Stadtplätzen direkt verbunden sind. Damit wird der ursprüngliche und über lange Zeiträume bewahrte Charakter der Höfe als öffentliche Plätze bestätigt und weiterentwickelt, der in den Gemälden Eduard Gaertners aus den ersten Jahrzehnten des 19. Jahrhunderts gut dokumentiert ist.

Schlüterhof: Mit seinen Triumphportalen und den sie umgebenden Loggien scheint der rekonstruierte, 50 Meter breite und 80 Meter lange Schlüterhof von der *piazza ideale* inspiriert zu sein, die in den Traktaten

Le corti come Luoghi pubblici

Il vecchio Castello aveva due corti, il nuovo ne ha tre: il ricostruito e completato *Schlüterhof*, il *Passage* e il *Foyer*. Le due nuove corti, ricavate nell'area dell'Eosanderhof – un'area che secondo il Bando poteva essere completamente edificata –, sono state messe in relazione con i suoi tre portali, e quindi in diretto collegamento con le piazze della città. A conferma e sviluppo del loro originario, e a lungo mantenuto, carattere di luogo pubblico, ben illustrato ancora nei primi decenni dell'Ottocento nei dipinti di Eduard Gaertner.

Schlüterhof: con i suoi portali trionfali e le logge che l'attorniano, la corte ricostruita, larga 50 e lunga 80 metri, sembra esser stata ispirata dalla *piazza ideale*, descritta nei trattati di Leon Battista Alberti e Andrea Palladio. Su tre lati sono ritornate le facciate barocche, disegnate da Schlüter; sul quarto lato si trova un

The courtyards as public Places

The old Palace had two courtyards, the new one has three: the reconstructed and completed *Schlüterhof*, the *Passage* and *Foyer*. The two new courtyards, created in the area of the Eosanderhof – an area that according to the competition program could be completely built on –, were placed in relation to its three portals, and thus in direct connection with the squares of the city. This confirms and develops their original, and long maintained, character as public places, well illustrated even in the first decades of the 19th century in the paintings of Eduard Gaertner.

Schlüterhof: with its triumphal portals and loggias surrounding it, the reconstructed courtyard, 50 metres wide and 80 metres long, seems to be inspired by the *piazza ideale* described in the treatises by Leon Battista Alberti and Andrea Palladio. On three sides the Baroque façades designed by Schlüter have returned;

Schlüterhof

Blick auf die rekonstruierten Ost- und Nordfassaden und die neue Westfassade

Veduta delle ricostruite facciate est e nord e della nuova facciata ovest

View of the reconstructed east and north façades and the new west façade

Blick auf die Passage aus dem Atrium des rekonstruierten südlichen Portals

Vista del Passage dall'atrio del ricostruito Portale sud

View of the Passage from the atrium of the reconstructed south Portal

Leon Battista Albertis und Andrea Palladios beschrieben wird. Auf drei Seiten kehrten die von Schlüter entworfenen Barockfassaden zurück, auf der vierten Seite wurde ein neuer Baukörper errichtet, der dem von Schlüter vorgesehenen, doch nicht realisierten Bau analog ist, der das vorbarocke »Quergebäude« ersetzen sollte.

Seine Fassade ist, wie die der drei rekonstruierten Seiten, durch das Motiv der steinernen Loggien in den unteren und das Motiv der verputzten Fensterwand in den beiden oberen Geschossen geprägt. Alt und Neu teilen sich die Aufgabe, diesem Hof, der einst Ort des höfischen Zeremoniells war und heute wieder derjenige von Theater- und Musikaufführungen werden soll, den szenografischen Charakter eines *Theaterplatzes* zu verleihen.

Der Blick durch die stets offenen Portale in der Mitte der kurzen Seiten trifft im Norden auf die tempelartige Fassade der Alten Nationalgalerie und im Süden auf das Gebäude des ehemaligen Marstalls.

nuovo corpo di fabbrica, analogo a quello previsto, ma non realizzato, in sostituzione del preesistente «edificio trasversale».

La sua facciata, così come quelle ricostruite, è caratterizzata dal motivo delle logge di pietra nei due piani inferiori, e della parete finestrata intonacata nei due piani superiori. Antico e Nuovo condividono il compito di conferire a questa corte – in origine luogo del cerimoniale e oggi di eventi teatrali e musicali – il carattere scenografico della *piazza-teatro*.

La vista attraverso i portali sempre aperti, disposti al centro dei lati minori, trova il suo punto di arrivo nella facciata-tempio della Alte Nationalgalerie a nord, e nella Marstall, le scuderie dell'antico Castello, a sud.

Passage: Una pubblica 'via colonnata' attraversa l'edificio lungo l'asse mediano nord-sud, collegando i contrapposti portali ricostruiti, che sono sempre stati i luoghi dell'entrata e dell'uscita del Castello. E' de-

on the fourth side is a newly built building, similar to the one he planned but did not realise, replacing the existing "transverse building".

Its façade, like the reconstructed ones, is characterised by the motif of the stone loggias on the two lower floors, and the plastered window wall on the two upper floors. Old and Modern share the purpose of giving this courtyard – originally the ceremonial place and now a place for theatrical and musical events – the scenic character of the *piazza-theatre*.

The view through the always open portals, situated in the middle of the smaller sides, finds its end point in the 'Greek colonnade' of the Alte Nationalgalerie to the north, and in the Marstall, the stables of the former Palace, to the south.

Passage: A public 'colonnaded way' traverses the building along the north-south median axis, connecting the reconstructed portals, which have always been the entrance and the exit of the Palace. It is bordered

Passage

Blick auf die neue *via colonnata* und das rekonstruierte Portal IV. Im Hintergrund: die Kolonnade des Alten Museums

Vista della nuova *via colonnata* e del ricostruito portale IV. Sul fondo: il colonnato dell'Altes Museum

View of the new *via colonnata* and the reconstructed Portal IV. In the background: the colonnade of the Altes Museum

Der einstige Eosanderhof: Detail des Gemäldes von Eduard Gaertner, um 1830

Il precedente Eosanderhof: Dettaglio del dipinto di Eduard Gaertner, intorno al 1830

The former Eosanderhof: Detail of painting by Eduard Gaertner, around 1830

Foyer

Blick auf das rekonstruierte Portal III und die neuen Loggien

Veduta del ricostruito Portale III e dei nuovi loggiati

View of the reconstructed Portal III and the new loggias

Passage: Eine öffentliche ›via colonnata‹ (Kolonnadenweg) durchquert das Gebäude entlang der nord-südlich ausgerichteten Mittelachse und verbindet die einander gegenüberstehenden rekonstruierten Portale, die seit je die Ein- und Ausgänge des Schlosses waren. Die Passage ist von zwei neuen linearen Baukörpern begrenzt, deren gleiche Fassaden durch drei übereinanderliegende Säulenordnungen geschmückt sind, sodass dieser Ort an ein römisch-antikes Forum erinnert.

Wie bei den Uffizien in Florenz ist ein in der Mitte des Gebäudes liegender Hof auch ein Platz im Zentrum der Stadt: Die jeweiligen Höhen- und Breitenabmessungen sind fast die gleichen, obwohl sie, im Fall des Berliner Schlosses, von den rekonstruierten Portalen bestimmt sind. Das eindrucksvolle Bild der Kolonnade des Alten Museums im Nordportal und der Blick in die Breite Straße – eine der wichtigsten Straßen des mittelalterlichen Berlin – durch das Südportal führen die

limitata da nuovi corpi di fabbrica lineari, la cui facciata è adornata da tre ordini di colonne sovrapposti, talché questo luogo può ricordare l'antico Foro dei Romani.

Come nel caso degli Uffizi a Firenze, un cortile nel mezzo dell' edificio è anche una piazza nel centro della città: le rispettive misure di altezza e larghezza sono comparabili, anche se nel caso del Berliner Schloss sono dettate da quelle dei portali.

La suggestiva apparizione del fronte colonnato dell'Altes Museum nella veduta attraverso il portale nord, e della Breite Straße – una strada principale della scomparsa città medievale – attraverso il portale sud, fa rivivere l'esperienza dello stretto legame del Castello con la Città.

Foyer: Il luogo dell'ingresso e dell'accoglienza è una grande sala cubica di 30 metri di lato, predisposta anche per speciali feste e spettacoli d'arte varia. Ha una copertura vetrata, riquadrata da cassettoni me-

by new linear buildings, the façade of which is adorned with three superimposed orders of columns, so that this place may be reminiscent of the ancient Forum of the Romans.

As in the case of the Uffizi in Florence, a courtyard in the middle of the building is also a square in the centre of the city: the measurements of height and width are almost the same, although in the case of the Berlin Palace they are dictated by those of the portals.

The suggestive appearance of the colonnaded front of the Altes Museum in the view through the north portal, and of the Breite Straße – a main street of the lost medieval city – through the south portal, brings to life the experience of the Palace's close relation with the City.

Foyer: The entrance and reception place is a large cubic hall measuring 30 metres on a side, which is also prepared for special festivities and various art shows. It has a glass roof, framed by metal coffers. On the western side is the grandiose portal

Foyer

Blick auf das rekonstruierte Portal III und die neuen Loggien

Veduta del ricostruito Portale III e dei nuovi loggiati

View of the reconstructed Portal III and the new loggias

Foyer

Blick auf die neuen Loggien aus dem rekonstruierten Portal III

Veduta dei nuovi loggiati dal ricostruito Portale III

View of the new loggias from the reconstructed Portal III

enge Verbindung des Schlosses mit der Stadt wieder lebendig vor Augen.

Foyer: Der Eingangs- und Empfangsbereich ist ein kubischer Saal mit einer Seitenlänge von 30 Metern, der für festliche Veranstaltungen und gelegentlich für spezielle Aufführungen genutzt werden kann. Er ist versehen mit einem Glasdach, welches mit Metallkassetten abgeviert ist. An die Westseite ist das von Eosander entworfene großartige Portal zurückgekehrt, das dem römischen Triumphbogen des Konstantin nachempfunden wurde; die anderen drei Seiten präsentieren sich in Form von übereinanderliegenden Loggien. Das Zusammenspiel von Alt und Neu evoziert mit dem rekonstruierten Triumphbogen als Bühnenfront – analog der *scenae frons* von Palladios Teatro Olimpico in Vicenza – und den Loggien als Zuschauerlogen das Bild des Theaters.

tallici. Sul lato occidentale si ritrova il grandioso portale disegnato da Eosander, a imitazione dell'arco trionfale romano di Costantino; gli altri tre lati si presentano in forma di loggiati sovrapposti. La combinazione di Antico e Nuovo ricorda il teatro, con il ricostruito arco trionfale come fronte di scena – analogo allo *scenae frons* del palladiano Teatro Olimpico di Vicenza – e le gallerie come palchi per gli spettatori.

designed by Eosander, in imitation of the Roman triumphal Arch of Constantine; the other three sides are in the form of superimposed loggias. The combination of Old and New remind the theatre, with the reconstructed triumphal arch as the scene wall – analogous to the *scenae frons* of Palladio's Teatro Olimpico in Vicenza – and the galleries as spectator boxes.

Das zerstörte Portal IV nach der November-
revolution 1918: Die vom Architrav getragenen
Portalsäulen

Il distrutto Portale IV dopo la Rivoluzione di
Novembre del 1918: Le colonne del Portale
sostenute dall'architrave

The destroyed Portal IV after the November
Revolution of 1918: The Portal colum ms carried
by the architrave

Die Fassade aus Mauern und Säulen

Sowohl die rekonstruierten barocken wie auch die neuen Fassaden zeigen sich als Kombination von Mauern und Säulen, denen unterschiedliche Aufgaben zugewiesen werden: die Mauern stehen für die eigentliche Konstruktion, die Säulen - beziehungsweise architektonischen Ordnungen - für das ›Ornament‹.

Die ›Magie‹ der Säulenordnung besteht darin, dass sie den Trilith, die uralte Figur der *Drei-Steine* - zwei aufrecht stehenden und einem aufliegenden -, ins Gedächtnis ruft. Er versinnbildlicht die Dramaturgie des *Tragens* und *Lastens* und damit das ›Wunder‹ des menschlichen Genies, das sich über das Naturgesetz der Schwerkraft hinwegsetzen kann.

Diese fundamentale Bedeutung bleibt erhalten, auch wenn die Säule auf stilistische Eigenheiten wie Basis oder Kapitell, Entasis und Kanneluren oder sogar die Rundung verzichtet (eine Säule kann auch quadratisch sein), analog kann das Gebälk

La facciata di Muri e Colonne

La facciata, sia l'antica che la nuova, presenta spesso la combinazione di muri e colonne, con compiti distinti: al muro spetta la costruzione vera e propria, alle colonne, ovvero agli ordini architettonici, l''ornamento'.

La 'magia' degli ordini delle colonne consiste, io penso, nell'evocazione del Trilite, l'ancestrale figura delle *Tre Pietre* - due ritte in piedi e l'altra appoggiata sopra di esse - che rappresenta la drammaturgia del *portare* e dell'*essere portato*, e perciò il 'miracolo' del genio umano che inganna la legge di gravità della Natura.

Questo fondamentale significato si conserva anche quando la colonna rinuncia alle sue peculiarità stilistiche: alla base e al capitello, all'entasi e alle scanalature, financo alla sua rotondità (una colonna può essere anche quadrata); analogamente anche quando la trabeazione rinuncia al fregio e alla cornice e si riduce all'architrave.

The façade of Walls and Columns

The façade, both old and new, often presents a combination of walls and columns, with distinct roles: the wall for the actual construction, and the columns - i.e. the architectural orders - for the 'ornament'.

The 'magic' of the orders of the columns consists, I think, in the evocation of the Trilite, that is, the ancestral figure of the *Three Stones* - two standing upright and the other resting on top - which depicts the dramaturgy of *carrying* and *being carried*, the 'wonder' of the human genius that tricks Nature's law of gravity.

This fundamental signification is preserved even when the column renounces its stylistic peculiarities - the base and capital, the entablature and fluting, even its roundness (a column can also be square); similarly when the entablature renounces the frieze and cornice and is reduced to the architrave.

Completely superfluous to the construction of the house, that is of

Passage

Die vor der tragenden Wand errichtete Kolonnade

Il colonnato antistante la parete portante

The colonnade in front of the supporting wall

auf Fries und Gesims verzichten und auf den Architrav reduziert werden.

Die Säulenordnung ist für den Hausbau, also für den Bau eines bewohnbaren, geschützten und überdachten Raums, überflüssig. Doch war sie zu allen Zeiten der Architekturgeschichte das wichtigste Mittel zur Hervorhebung der Götterhäuser und unzähliger religiöser wie profaner Bauwerke. Man denke an die vor den Mauern der antiken Tempel, Agoren und Foren errichteten Kolonnaden sowie an die Halbsäulen beziehungsweise Pilaster, die zuerst an den wichtigsten öffentlichen Gebäuden Roms (das bekannteste Beispiel ist das Kolosseum) und seit der Renaissance auch an den Fassaden von Kirchen und öffentlichen und privaten Palästen angebracht wurden.

Um die außerordentliche Bedeutung der Säulenordnung geht es Leon Battista Alberti, wenn er schreibt, dass »in der gesamten Geschichte der Architektur das grundlegende Ornament zweifellos die Säulen sind.«[7] Dies galt auch lange Zeit nach Alberti, bis die architektonische Ord-

Del tutto superfluo per la costruzione della casa, ovvero di uno spazio abitabile recintato e coperto, l'ordine delle colonne è stato invece in tutti i tempi della storia dell'architettura il principale mezzo per mettere in risalto le case degli dei, e poi anche innumerevoli edifici, religiosi e profani. Si pensi ai colonnati eretti davanti ai muri degli antichi Templi, Agora e Fori, ma anche alle semicolonne e alle lesene, dapprima applicate ai muri dei principali edifici pubblici romani (l'esempio più famoso è il Colosseo) e dal Rinascimento anche alle facciate delle chiese e di numerosi palazzi pubblici e privati.

Della straordinaria importanza degli ordini architettonici parla Leon Battista Alberti quando scrive: «in tutta la storia dell'architettura, l'ornamento fondamentale è costituito senza dubbio dalle colonne.»[7] Ciò vale anche per molto tempo dopo Alberti, fino all'eclisse degli ordini architettonici nell'architettura moderna del secolo scorso.

Nell'architettura contemporanea di Berlino, l'ordine architettonico è

an enclosed and covered habitable space, the order of the columns has instead been at all times in the history of architecture the principal means of highlighting the houses of the gods, and then also of numerous buildings, both religious and profane. One thinks of the colonnades erected in front of the walls of the ancient Temples, Agoras and Forums, but also of the half-columns and pilasters, first applied to the walls of the main Roman public buildings (the most famous example is the Colosseum) and since the Renaissance also to the façades of churches and numerous public and private palaces.

Leon Battista Alberti speaks of the extraordinary importance of architectural orders when he writes: "in the entire history of architecture, the fundamental ornamentation is undoubtedly columns."[7] This is also true for a long time after Alberti, until the eclipse of architectural orders in modern architecture in the last century.

In contemporary Berlin architecture, the architectural order is evoked

Neuer Spreeflügel:
Die von der hinteren Wand getragene trilithische Fassade

Nuova ala sulla Sprea:
La facciata trilitica portata dalla parete retrostante

New wing towards the Spree:
The trilithic façade supported from the wall behind

nung in der modernen Baukunst des letzten Jahrhunderts verschwand.

In der zeitgenössischen Berliner Architektur wird die Säulenordnung hauptsächlich auf zweierlei Art evoziert: durch die Inszenierung einer von konstruktiven Aufgaben befreiten Tektonik, mit der die Fassade nach ›menschlichen‹ Proportionen gegliedert wird, und durch Pfeilerreihen vor die das Innen vom Außen trennenden Wände gestellt, die an Tempelkolonnaden erinnern. Zum ersten Mal nach dem Zweiten Weltkrieg wurde die Tempelfigur in Berlin von der Neuen Nationalgalerie Mies van der Rohes wachgerufen, auch dank Pfeilern, die durch ihre einzigartige Stellung und Form an Säulen erinnern.

Beim Berliner Schloss führte die Suche nach einer modernen Formensprache im harmonischen Dialog mit der barocken schließlich zur zeitlosen Sprache des Triliths.

Der Bezug der Säulen zu der jeweils dahinterliegenden Wand ist unterschiedlich. In den rekonstruierten Loggien des Schlüterhofs und in den

evocato principalmente in due diversi modi: attraverso la messa in scena di una tettonica che, liberata di compiti costruttivi, ripartisce la facciata in proporzioni 'a scala umana', e attraverso file di pilastri, disposti davanti alle pareti che separano l'interno dall'esterno, che richiamano le colonne del tempio. La figura del tempio è stata evocata per la prima volta a Berlino nel Dopoguerra dalla Nationalgalerie di Mies van der Rohe, anche grazie a pilastri che per disposizione e forma ricordano le colonne.

Nel caso del Castello di Berlino, la ricerca di un linguaggio moderno in dialogo armonioso con quello barocco è infine, approdata al linguaggio senza tempo del Trilite.

Molteplici sono le modalità di relazione delle colonne con il muro retrostante. Nelle logge ricostruite dello Schlüterhof, e nelle nuove gallerie del Foyer, le colonne - tonde e binate nel primo caso, quadrate nel secondo - sono disposte a una distanza tale dal muro da conformare un corridoio. Nei portali ricostruiti

mainly in two different ways: through the mise en scene of a tectonics that, freed of construction tasks, reparts the façade in 'human-scale' proportions, and through rows of pillars, disposed in front of the walls separating the interior from the exterior, that recall temple columns. The figure of the temple was first evoked in post-war Berlin by Mies van der Rohe's Nationalgalerie, also thank to pillars whose disposition and form are reminiscent of columns.

In the case of the Berlin Palace, the search for a modern language in harmonious dialogue with the Baroque one finally led to the timeless language of Trilite.

There are many ways in which the columns relate to the wall behind them. In the reconstructed loggias of the Schlüterhof, and in the new galleries of the Foyer, the columns – round and paired in the first case, square in the second – are positioned at the distance of a corridor from the wall.

In the reconstructed portals of the west and south façades and the

Café-Restaurant auf dem Dach:
Die von der hinteren Pfeilerwand getragene trilithische Fassade

Café-Restaurant sul tetto:
La facciata trilitica portata dalla retrostante parete di pilastri

Café-Restaurant on the roof:
The trilithic façade carried by a wall of pillars behind

neuen Galerien des Foyers stehen die Säulen – im ersten Fall rund und paarweise, im zweiten Fall quadratisch – in einem solchen Abstand vor der Wand, dass sich ein Durchgang ergibt. In den rekonstruierten Portalen der West- und Südfassade und des Schlüterhofs sowie in den neuen Fassaden der Passage stehen die Säulen sehr nahe an der Wand; in den rekonstruierten Portalen der Nordfassade sind es Lisenen. Auch die Fassaden des neuen Spreeflügels und des Pavillon-Restaurants auf dem Dach sind als Trilithen-Reihe konzipiert: Im ersten Fall hat das System eine konstruktive wie auch ornamentale Funktion, im zweiten Fall wird es von einer dahinterliegenden Konstruktion aus Stahl und Beton getragen.

Vielleicht hatte Goethe die herausragende symbolische, um nicht zu sagen metaphysische Bedeutung der Säule intuitiv erfasst, als er in Bezug auf Palladios Bauten, die er in Vicenza gesehen hatte, ausführte: »Die höchste Schwierigkeit, mit der dieser Mann wie alle neuern Archi-

delle facciate ovest e sud e dello Schlüterhof, e nelle nuove facciate del Passage, le colonne sono vicinissime al muro; nei portali ricostruiti della facciata nord sono invece lesene direttamente applicate al muro. Anche le facciate del nuovo fronte sulla Sprea e del padiglione-ristorante sul tetto sono pensate come un'addizione di triliti: nel primo caso, sono al tempo stesso costruzione e ornamento; nel secondo, sono appesi a una simile struttura retrostante di ferro e cemento.

Forse Goethe aveva intuito l'eminente significato simbolico, per non dire metafisico, della colonna, quando, riferendosi agli edifici di Palladio che aveva appena visto a Vicenza, arriva a dire: «Nell'architettura civile la maggior difficoltà sta sempre nella disposizione degli ordini di colonne; collegare colonne e muri rimane pur sempre una contraddizione. Ma con quale perizia egli [Palladio, *n.d.s.*] ha saputo associare il tutto, com'è riuscito ad imporsi con l'immanenza delle sue opere, facendo dimenticare quanto

Schlüterhof, and in the new façades of the Passage, the columns are very close to the wall; in the reconstructed portals of the north façade, however, they are pilasters directly applied to the wall. The façades of the new front on the Spree and the pavilion-restaurant on the roof are also conceived as an addition of trilites: in the first case, they are both construction and ornament; in the second, they are supported by a similar iron structure behind them.

Perhaps Goethe understood the eminent symbolic, not to say metaphysical, significance of the column when, referring to Palladio's buildings he had just seen in Vicenza, he went so far as to say: "In civil architecture, the greatest difficulty always lies in the arrangement of the orders of columns; connecting columns and walls is almost impossible, if one does not possess skill. But with what skill he [Palladio, *author's note*] was able to combine everything, how he managed to impose himself with the immanence of his works, making us forget how much is disproportionate

Passage:
Details der neuen Fassade
Dettagli della nuova facciata
Details of the new façade

AUSSENANSICHT

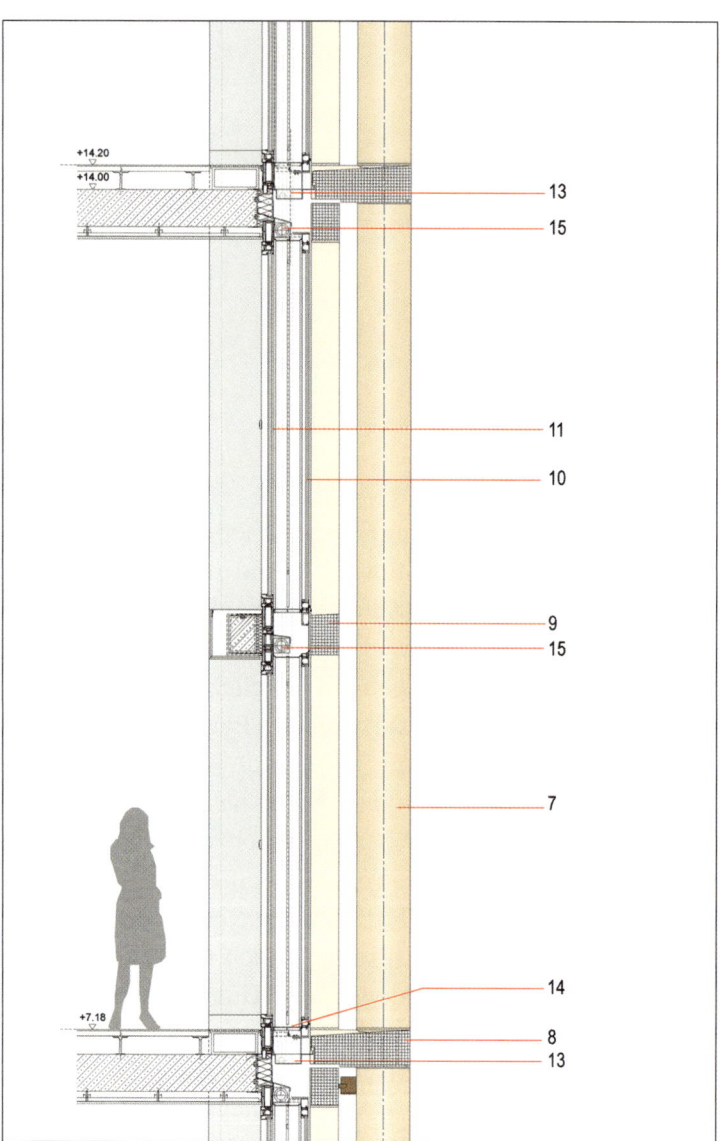

SCHNITT

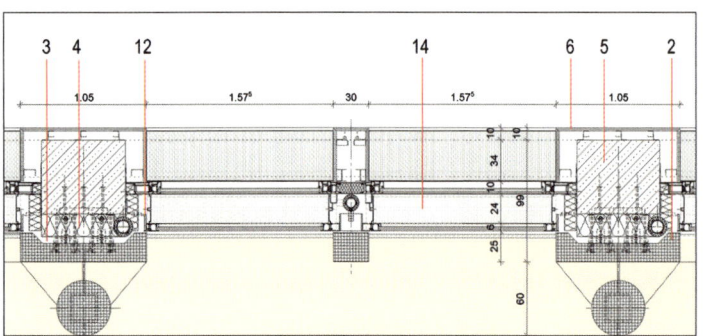

GRUNDRISS

Wandaufbau Neue Fassade
1 Lasur Hydrophobierung, Farbton: farblos
2 Fertigteilelement Architekturbeton, 150 bis 250mm
   Oberfläche gesäuert, Farbton: wie Sandstein
3 Luftschicht, 50mm
4 Mineralische Dämmung, 180mm
5 Wandpfeiler Stahlbeton, 600mm
6 Innenwand Trockenbau Gips, 100mm

Weiteres:
7 Säule Architekturbeton, 450mm
8 Architrav Architekturbeton,
   mit Innengefälle, 300mm x 850mm
9 Fensterkreuz Architekturbeton

Fenster Neue Fassade
Kastenfenster Metall, bestehend aus:
10 Aussenfenster Stahl
   Verbundsicherheitsglas, absturzsichernd
11 Innenfenster Aluminium
   Wärmeschutz-/ Sicherheitsverglasung
   Fugendichtheitsklasse IV

Weiteres:
Fensterfarbton: Marrone Glimmer
12 Stahleinbauzarge, feuerverzinkt, mineralisch gedämmt
13 Entwässerungsrinne Fenster und Architrav,
   Aluminium beschichtet
14 Abdeckrost, Stahl beschichtet
15 Sonnenschutzbehang, motorisch verfahrbar
   Textilbehang, transparent

tekten zu kämpfen hatte, ist die schickliche Anwendung der Säulenordnungen in der bürgerlichen Baukunst; denn Säulen und Mauern zu verbinden, bleibt doch immer ein Widerspruch. Aber wie er das untereinander gearbeitet hat, wie er durch die Gegenwart seiner Werke imponiert und vergessen macht, daß er nur überredet! Es ist wirklich etwas Göttliches in seinen Anlagen, völlig wie die Force des großen Dichters, der aus Wahrheit und Lüge ein Drittes bildet, dessen erborgtes Dasein uns bezaubert.«[8] Darin äußert sich die Faszination von einer Idee der Architektur als ›zeitbedingte Konstruktion‹ und zugleich als ›zeitlose Repräsentation der Konstruktion‹: einer Architektur zum Wohnen und zur Betrachtung.

Die bauliche Einfassung des rekonstruierten Teils ist eine dreischichtige Konstruktion, deren Dicke mit derjenigen der Mauer des alten Schlosses korrespondiert: Die innere Schicht ist eine tragende Stahlbetonwand mit einer Dicke von 30 bis 50 Zentimetern, die mittlere

c'è in loro di spropositato. C'è veramente qualcosa di divino nelle sue strutture, c'è tutta la forza del grande poeta che dalla verità e dalla menzogna ricava un terzo elemento, che ci affascina.»[8] E' il fascino di un'idea di architettura come 'costruzione dipendente dal tempo', e come 'rappresentazione della costruzione senza tempo': un'architettura da abitare e da contemplare.

Il recinto edilizio della parte ricostruita è una costruzione a tre strati, con uno spessore comparabile a quello dei muri del vecchio Castello: lo strato interno è un muro portante di cemento armato, di spessore variabile da 30 a 50 cm, quello intermedio è uno strato di isolamento termico di 12 cm, quello esterno è un muro di mattoni di spessore medio di 65 cm, con numerosi inserti di pietra, intonacato e dipinto color avorio. La parete, a cui specificamente si riferisce il termine di facciata barocca è dunque un muro autoportante senza giunti di dilatazione in vista, e non un rivestimento di pannelli prefabbricati di mattoni,

in them. There is really something divine in his structures, there is all the strength of the great poet who derives a third element from truth and lies, which fascinates us."[8] It is the fascination of an idea of 'architecture as 'time-dependent construction' and as a 'representation of the timeless construction': an architecture to be inhabit and to be contemplated.

The built enclosure of the reconstructed part is a three-layer construction, with a thickness comparable to that of the walls of the old Palace: the inner layer is a carrying wall of reinforced concrete, with thickness varies from 30 to 50 cm, the intermediate layer is a 12 cm layer of thermal insulation, and the outer layer is a brick wall with an average thickness of 65 cm, with numerous stone inserts, plastered and painted ivory. The wall, to which the term Baroque façade specifically refers, is thus a self-supporting wall with no visible expansion joints, and not a covering of prefabricated brick panels, hanged from a structure behind,

Die rekonstruierte Fassade im Bau
La facciata ricostruita a lavori in corso
The reconstructed façade during its construction

ist eine 12 Zentimeter dicke Wärmedämmplatte, die äußere eine durchschnittlich 65 Zentimeter dicke Ziegelmauerwand mit zahlreichen Steineinlagen, die verputzt und elfenbeinfarben gestrichen ist. Die Wand, auf die sich der Begriff Barockfassade spezifisch bezieht, ist also eine selbsttragende Konstruktion ohne sichtbare Dehnungsfugen, keine Verkleidung aus vorgefertigten Ziegelplatten, die an einer dahinterliegenden Tragstruktur hängen, wie es bei Gebäuden ähnlicher Größe seit langem und meist der Fall ist. Die Säulen und Architrave, die Fensterrahmen und alle anderen Verzierungen wurden aus Sandsteinstücken gefügt, deren Größe und Form möglichst nahe an den Originalen sind.

Die bauliche Einfassung des neuen Teils ist ebenfalls dreischichtig und unterscheidet sich von den rekonstruierten durch eine Verkleidung aus großen Steinplatten und durch monolithische Säulen und Architrave, die aus einer Mischung aus Sandstein und Weißzement bestehen.

appesi a una struttura retrostante, come da tempo avviene nelle costruzioni di simili dimensioni. Le colonne e gli architravi, le cornici delle finestre e ogni altro decoro, sono stati ricostruiti assemblando pezzi di pietra arenaria, di dimensione e forma il più possibile uguali a quelle originali.

Anche il recinto edilizio della parte nuova è tripartito e si distingue da quello ricostruito per il rivestimento delle pareti con grandi lastre e per le colonne e gli architravi monolitici, ottenuti da una miscela di pietra arenaria e cemento bianco.

as has long been the case in buildings of similar size. The columns and architraves, window frames and all other decoration have been reconstructed by assembling pieces of sandstone, of the same size and form as the original as far as possible.

The built enclosure of the new part is also tripartite and differs from the reconstructed one by the walls covered with large slabs and monolithic columns and architraves, made from a mixture of sandstone and white cement.

Werkstatt der Skulpturen (Bauhütte):
Statuenmodelle aus Gips für die Rekonstruktion aus Stein

Laboratorio delle Sculture (Bauhütte):
Modelli di statue in gesso per la ricostruzione in pietra

Sculpture workshop (Bauhütte):
Models of plaster statues for stone reconstruction

Die Skulpturen

Bei den Statuen über Säulen oder in Nischen sowie bei den Hochreliefs und Skulpturengruppen über den Hauptportalen: In allen Fällen handelte es sich um Kunstwerke, die auf den bestimmten Ort bezogen waren, anders als diejenigen, die man in den Museen findet, welche für einen anderen oder für keinen speziellen Ort vorgesehen waren. Man kann sagen, dass die Skulptur am Schloss integraler Bestandteil eines als *Gesamtkunstwerk* verstandenen Gebäudes war.

Bis auf wenige restaurierte Originalfragmente wurden alle Skulpturen im Außenbereich auf Grundlage von Spolien, Zeichnungen, Fotografien sowie literarischen Quellen vollständig rekonstruiert und wieder dort aufgestellt, wo sie waren.

Einige Statuen oder Hochreliefs sind Unikate, die von der Hand eines Bildhauers geschaffen wurden; andere wie Friese, Gesimse, Kapitelle oder Balustraden, insgesamt etwa dreitausend Stück, wurden anhand

Le sculture

Statue sopra le colonne o dentro le nicchie, altorilievi e gruppi scultorei sopra le porte principali: in ogni caso si trattava di opere d'arte pensate in relazione a un luogo ben preciso, diversamente ad esempio da quelle che normalmente si trovano nei Musei, quasi sempre pensate per un altro o per nessun luogo in particolare. Si può dire che la scultura nel Castello era parte integrante di un edificio concepito come *opera d'arte totale*.

Ad eccezione di pochi frammenti restaurati, tutte le sculture che si trovano all'esterno sono state ricostruite nella loro originale interezza, sulla base di frammenti, disegni, foto e fonti letterarie.

Alcune, come le statue o gli altorilievi, sono pezzi unici, fatti dalla mano di uno scultore; le altre, come i fregi e le cornici, i capitelli o le balaustre: circa tremila pezzi – a partire da trecento modelli, prima in argilla e poi in gesso – sono stati fatti a macchina e infine rifiniti in-

The sculptures

Statues above the columns or inside the niches, high reliefs and sculptural groups above the main doors: in each case, these were works of art conceived in relation to a specific place, unlike, for example, those normally found in museums, which are almost always conceived for another or no place in particular. It can be said that the sculpture in the Berlin Palace was an integral part of a building conceived as a *total work of art*.

With the exception of a few restored fragments, all the sculptures outside have been reconstructed in their original entirety, based on fragments, drawings, photos and literary sources.

Some, such as the statues or high reliefs, are unique pieces, made by the hand of a sculptor; the others, such as the friezes and cornices, capitals or balustrades, some three thousand pieces – starting from three hundred models, first in clay and then in gypsum – were made by machine, and finally individually

Werkstatt der Skulpturen (Bauhütte):
Gipsmodell einer Skulpturgruppe für deren
Rekonstruktion aus Stein

Laboratorio delle Sculture (Bauhütte):
Modello in gesso di un gruppo scultoreo
per la sua ricostruzione in pietra

Sculpture workshop (Bauhütte):
Plaster model of a sculptural group for
its stone reconstruction

von über dreihundert Modellen zunächst in Ton und dann in Gips maschinell hergestellt und zuletzt von der Hand eines Steinmetzen individuell bearbeitet.

Die künstlerisch äußerst wertvollen Skulpturen, die zu empfindlich sind, um in den Außenbereich zurückzukehren, wurden unter Beibehaltung ihres heutigen Zustands restauriert und sind nun in den Innenräumen aufgestellt. Dabei handelt es sich um unterschiedlich stark beschädigte Figuren, die von einer nicht mehr zu entfernenden Patina der Zeit geschwärzt sind.

Unter ihnen sind von besonderem Wert die Statuen, die von Schlüter selbst und den Mitarbeitern seiner Werkstatt gehauen wurden – der Architekt des Barockschlosses war auch ein berühmter Bildhauer, der als »Michelangelo des Nordens« gepriesen wurde. Die Statuen standen im Freien auf den Kolossalsäulen des großen Portals im Schlüterhof und befinden sich nun im Skulpturensaal, in einer der äußeren analogen inneren Fassade, abermals auf Säu-

dividualmente dalla mano di uno scalpellino.

Le sculture di maggiore valore artistico, troppo vulnerabili per ritornare all'esterno, sono state restaurate senza alterarne lo stato attuale e sono ora esposte all'interno. Si tratta di figure variamente mutilate, annerite da una patina del tempo che non può più essere rimossa.

Fra di esse, di particolare valore sono le statue scolpite da Schlüter – il primo architetto del Castello barocco era anche un famoso scultore, considerato il «Michelangelo del Nord» – e dai collaboratori della sua bottega. Stavano all'aperto sopra le colonne d'ordine gigante del grande portale dello Schlüterhof, si trovano adesso nella Sala delle Sculture, in una facciata interna analoga a quella esterna in cui stavano, ancora sopra colonne, ora colonne quadrate, appena distaccate dalla parete: si riproduce in tal modo anche un punto di vista simile a quello originario. Al loro posto, nello Schlüterhof, si trovano ora delle copie.

refinished by the hand of a stonemason.

The sculptures of greatest artistic value, which were too vulnerable to return to the outside world, were restored without altering their current state and are now exposed inside. These are variously mutilated figures, blackened by a patina of time that can no longer be removed.

Particularly valuable among them are the statues sculpted by Schlüter – the first architect of the Baroque palace was also a famous sculptor, considered the "Michelangelo of the North" – and his workshop assistants. They stood in the open air above the giant order columns of the Schlüterhof's great gateway, and are now in the Sculpture Hall, in an interior façade similar to the exterior, still above columns, now square columns, just detached from the wall: this also reproduces a viewpoint similar to the original one. Copies now stand in their place in the Schlüterhof.

Unique stone pieces and gypsum models for serial reproduction in

Werkstatt der Skulpturen (Bauhütte):
Kapitell in Restaurierung

Laboratorio delle Sculture (Bauhütte):
capitello in restauro

Sculpture workshop (Bauhütte):
capital under restauration

len, nun ›quadratischen Säulen‹, im geringen Abstand zu den Wänden: Damit wird ein Blick zurückgewonnen, der dem ursprünglichen ähnlich ist. An der Stelle, wo sie einst im Schlüterhof standen, sind Kopien aufgestellt.

Die steinernen Unikate sowie die Gipsmodelle der seriellen Reproduktion in Stein wurden von zahlreichen Bildhauern und Steinmetzen in der Schlossbauhütte angefertigt, die von Experten für barocke Bildhauerei unterstützt wurden.

Pezzi unici di pietra e modelli in gesso per la riproduzione seriale in pietra sono stati realizzati nella cosiddetta Schlossbauhütte da numerosi scultori e scalpellini, assistiti da esperti di scultura barocca.

stone were made in the so-called Schlossbauhütte by numerous sculptors and stonemasons, assisted by Baroque sculpture experts.

Skulpturensaal: die restaurierten Statuen
Schlüters und seiner Werkstatt

Sala delle Sculture: le statue restaurate
di Schlüter e della sua bottega

Sculpture Hall: the restored statues
of Schlüter and his workshop

Die Architektur des Berliner Schlosses – Humboldt Forums

L'architettura del Berliner Schloss – Humboldt Forum

The architecture of Berliner Schloss – Humboldt Forum

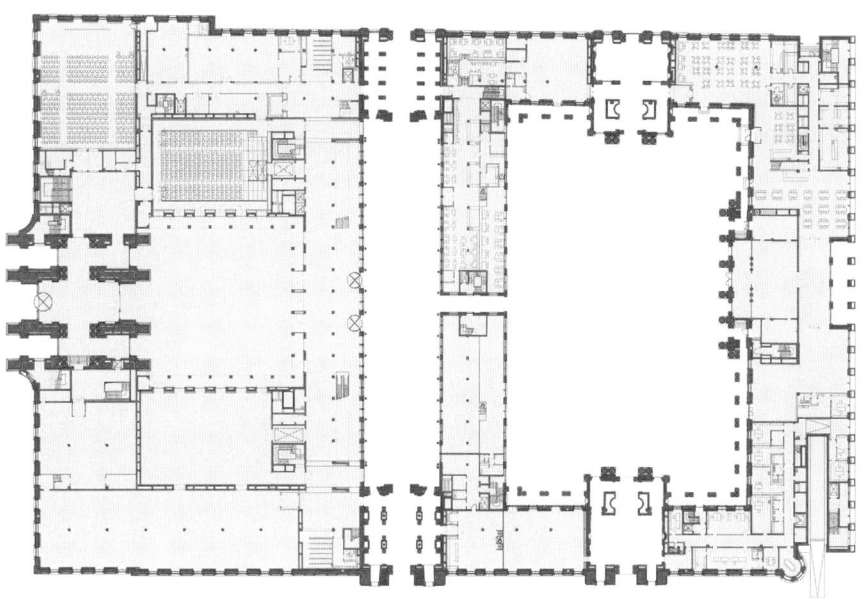

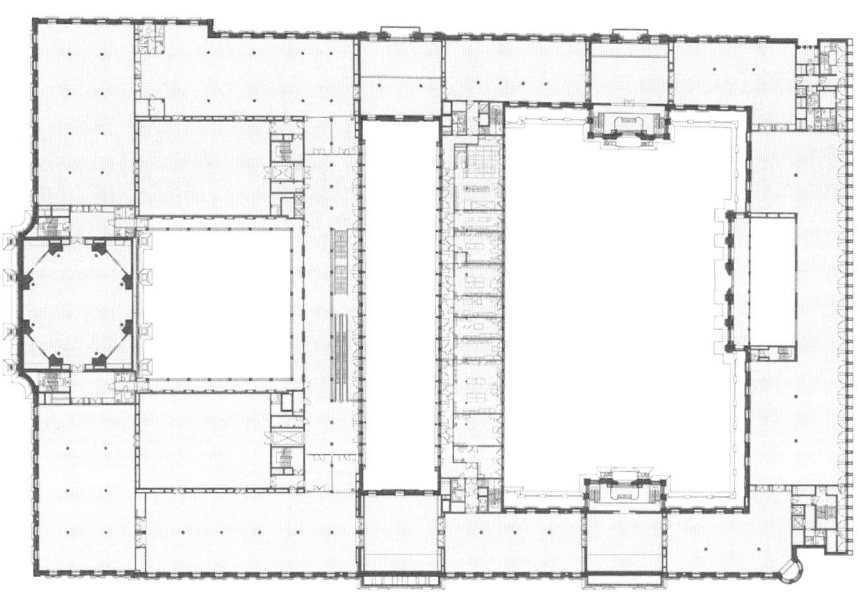

Grundriss Erdgeschoss (oben)
Grundriss 3. Obergeschoss (unten)

Pianta piano terra (sopra)
Pianta del terzo piano (sotto)

Ground floor plan (above)
Third floor plan (below)

Die Innenräume

Alle Innenräume bekamen eine neue und zweckmäßige Gestaltung sowie eine hochmoderne technische Ausrüstung. Bei der Anordnung der Pfeiler und Balken wurde darauf geachtet, die Möglichkeit einer zukünftigen Rekonstruktion der Räume von besonderem künstlerisch-historischem Wert nicht zu verbauen.

Die Gesamtnutzfläche von 40.000 Quadratmetern ist ungefähr zur Hälfte für die Ausstellung der ca. 20.000 Artefakte außereuropäischer Kulturen bestimmt, die aus den Staatlichen Museen in Dahlem hierhin überführt wurden. Ungefähr 10.000 Quadratmeter sind den Räumen allgemeiner öffentlicher Nutzung vorbehalten.

Das Erdgeschoss umfasst die Eingangs- und Treppenhalle, das große Foyer, das Auditorium und den Multifunktionssaal, die Säle für Wechselausstellungen und die Darstellung der Geschichte des Ortes, den Skulpturensaal sowie Buchhandlungen, Restaurants und Cafés.

Gli spazi interni

Tutti gli spazi interni sono stati ridisegnati in forme adeguate al loro nuovo scopo e attrezzati con i più moderni mezzi tecnici. La disposizione di pilastri e travi è attenta a non pregiudicare la possibilità di una futura ricostruzione dei luoghi di particolare valore storico-artistico.

Della superfice utile complessiva di 40.000 mq, circa una metà è destinata all'esposizione dei ventimila artefatti delle culture extraeuropee, qui trasferiti dai Musei Statali di Berlino-Dahlem; circa 10.000 mq sono destinati a spazi di interesse pubblico generale.

Nel piano terreno, si trovano la sala dell'ingresso e delle scale, il Foyer, l'auditorium e la sala multifunzionale, le sale per le mostre temporanee e la Storia del Luogo, la Sala della Scultura, i bookshops, ristoranti e caffè.

Nel primo piano, si trovano gli spazi per i Progetti culturali di Berlino e la Fondazione Stadtmuseum

The interior spaces

All the interior spaces have been redesigned and modernly equipped for their new purpose; the disposition of pillars and beams is careful not to prejudice the possibility of future reconstruction of spaces of particular historical and artistic value.

Of the total usable area of 40,000 square metres, about half is used for the exhibition of the 20,000 artefacts of non-European cultures, transferred here from the State Museums in Berlin-Dahlem, and about 10,000 square metres is used for spaces of general public interest.

On the ground floor, there is the entrance and staircase hall, the foyer, the auditorium and multifunctional hall, the rooms for temporary exhibitions and the History of the Place, the Sculpture Hall, bookshops, restaurants and cafés.

On the first floor, there are spaces for the Berlin Cultural Projects, Stadtmuseum Berlin Foundation, and for the collections of the Humboldt University; on the second and

Treppenhalle: Ansicht des Erdgeschosses

Sala delle Scale: veduta del piano terra

Hall of the Stairs: view of the ground floor

Treppenhalle: Blick aus der dritten Etage. Die ›schwarze Flagge‹ ist ein Werk des Künstlers Kang Sunkoo

Sala delle Scale: veduta dal terzo piano. La 'bandiera nera' è opera dell'artista Kang Sunkoo

Hall of the Stairs: view from the third floor. The 'black flag' is the work of the artist Kang Sunkoo

Ansicht einer Ausstellungshalle im neuen Spreeflügel

Veduta di una sala espositiva nella nuova ala verso la Sprea

View of an exhibition hall in the new wing facing the Spree

Ansicht der zweigeschosse-hohen Ausstellungshalle im neuen Baukörper, der sich mit Loggien zum Foyer hin öffnet

Veduta della sala espositiva a doppia altezza nel nuovo corpo di fabbrica che si affaccia con loggiati sul Foyer

View of the double-height exhibition hall in the new building opening with loggias onto the Foyer

Im ersten Obergeschoss befinden sich Räume für die Kulturprojekte Berlin und die Stiftung Stadtmuseum Berlin sowie die Sammlungen der Humboldt-Universität, im zweiten und dritten Obergeschoss das Ethnologische Museum und das Museum für Asiatische Kunst. Die Forschungslabore und Restaurierungswerkstätten sowie die Verwaltungs- und Betriebsbüros sind überwiegend in den östlichen Halbgeschossen entlang der Passage untergebracht. Der Keller erstreckt sich über das gesamte Grundstück: Auf einer öffentlichen Fläche von etwa 1.500 Quadratmetern liegen die Überreste der Keller des alten Schlosses; das übrige Areal des Untergeschosses und die Fläche des Dachgeschosses, im Ganzen 16.000 Quadratmeter, sind für Haustechnik und Depots bestimmt. Bei den Innenräumen war es nur meine Aufgabe, die ›feste Bühne‹ zu konzipieren, die durch in eigenen Wettbewerben ausgewählte Architekten und Designer mit mobilen Objekten, Einrichtungen für Ausstellungen und Beschilderungen ausgestattet wurden.

Berlin, e per le collezioni dell'Università Humboldt; nel secondo e terzo piano, gli spazi espositivi del Museo Etnologico e del Museo dell'Arte Asiatica. I laboratori di ricerca e di restauro, gli uffici amministrativi e tecnico-gestionali sono in prevalenza disposti nei mezzanini del nuovo edificio che delimita a est il Passage colonnato. Il piano sotterraneo si estende a tutto il lotto edificato: in un'area di circa 1.500 mq di pubblico accesso, si trovano i resti delle cantine dell'antico Castello; la superfice restante, ovvero quasi tutta, e l'intera superfice del piano sottotetto, per un totale di 16.000 mq, è destinata ai locali tecnici e ai depositi. Per quanto riguarda lo spazio interno, si deve al mio progetto la costruzione della 'scena fissa'; altri architetti e designer, scelti sulla base di specifici concorsi, hanno progettato gli elementi mobili, gli allestimenti espositivi e la segnaletica.

third floors are the exhibition spaces of the Ethnological Museum and the Museum of Asian Art. The research and restoration laboratories, administrative and technical-management offices are mainly located in the mezzanines of the new building bordering the colonnaded Passage to the east. The underground floor extends to the entire built plot: in an area of approximately 1,500 square metres of public access, the remains of the cellars of the former Palace are located; the remaining surface area, i. e. almost the entire surface area of the attic floor, a total of 16,000 square metres, is destined for technical rooms and storage areas. As far as the interior space is concerned, the construction of the 'fixed scene' is due to my design; other architects and designers, chosen on the basis of specific competitions, designed the movable elements, the exhibition layouts and the sign system.

Auditorium

Blick auf die Innenwand der rekonstruierten Westfassade

Vista verso la parete interna della ricostruita facciata ovest

View to the inner wall of the reconstructed west façade

Multifunktionssaal:
Ansicht mit Boden auf Terrainhöhe

Sala Multifunzionale:
vista con pavimento in posizione piana

Multipurpose Hall:
view with floor in flat position

Archäologisches Fenster:
Blicke auf die Überreste des Kellers des einstigen Schlosses

Finestra Archeologica:
vedute dei resti della cantina del vecchio Castello

Archaeological Window:
views of ruins of the cellar of the old Palace

Café-Restaurant auf dem Dach:
Ein Stadtloggia-ähnlicher Pavillon auf dem Dach

Caffè-Ristorante sul tetto:
Un padiglione simile a loggia urbana sul tetto

The Café-Restaurant on the roof:
A pavilion similar to an urban loggia on the roof

Die Stadt von der Dachterrasse aus gesehen

La città vista dalla terrazza sul tetto

The City as seen from the roof terrace

Das Dachrestaurant und die Dachterrasse

Auf der Dachfläche des nördlich gelegenen kubischen Neubaukörpers erhebt sich ein Pavillon in Form einer Stadtloggia, in dem sich ein Café-Restaurant befindet. Es ist von einer spektakulären, 1.500 Quadratmeter großen Terrasse umgeben, von der aus sich die nahen Baudenkmäler der historischen Mitte Berlins ›auf Augenhöhe‹ betrachten lassen.

Il Padiglione-ristorante e la Terrazza sul tetto

Sopra il piano di copertura del nuovo corpo cubico-nord si eleva un padiglione in forma di loggia urbana, dove si trova un caffè-ristorante. È attorniato da una spettacolare terrazza di 1.500 mq, da cui si possono ammirare 'ad altezza d'occhio' i vicini principali monumenti del Centro storico di Berlino.

The Pavilion-Restaurant and the Terrace on the roof

Above the roof plane of the new cubic-north building rises a pavilion in the form of an urban loggia, housing a café-restaurant. It is surrounded by a spectacular 1,500 square metre terrace, from which one can admire 'at eye level' the nearby main monuments of Berlin's historic centre.

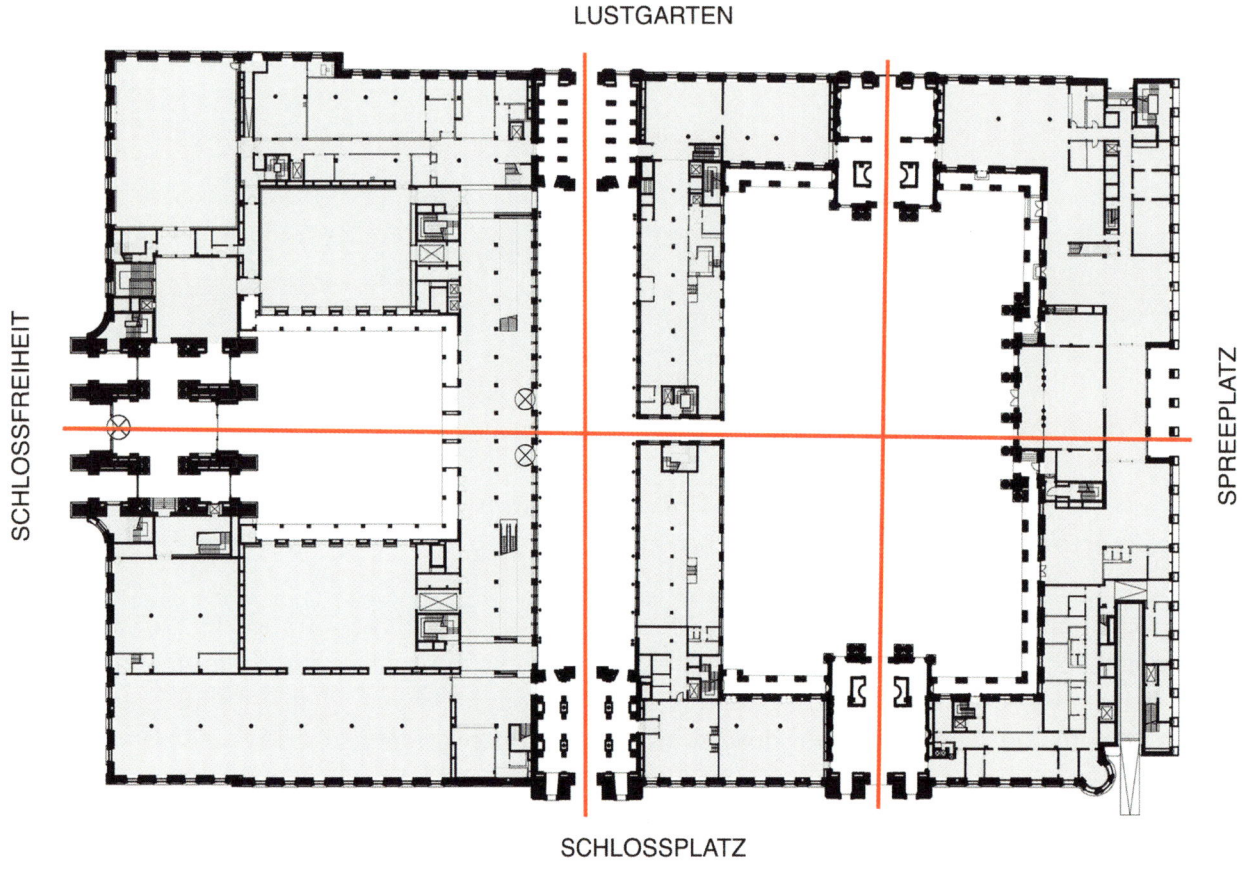

Grundriss Erdgeschoss:
Die öffentlichen Achsen, die das neue Schloss durchqueren

Pianta del piano terra:
Gli assi pubblici che attraversano il nuovo Castello

Plan of the ground floor:
the public axes that cross the new Palace

Die Große Piazza der Mitte Berlins

Dank der fünf Portale als Stadttore und der drei Höfe als öffentliche Plätze darf man das neue Berliner Schloss als eine *Stadt in Form eines Palastes* bezeichnen. Sie kann drei Millionen Besucher pro Jahr und täglich Tausende Berliner empfangen und schafft etwa 500 neue Arbeitsplätze.

Durch drei immer offene Portale und zwei öffentlich zugängliche Höfe vereinen sich die äußeren Plätze mit den inneren Höfen des neuen Berliner Schloss - Humboldt Forums zu einem einzigen öffentlichen Raum, den man als die *Große Piazza* der Mitte Berlins bezeichnen darf.

La Piazza Grande del Centro di Berlino

In virtù di cinque portali-porta di città e di tre corti-piazza, il nuovo Castello di Berlino si potrebbe definire una *città in forma di palazzo*, capace di accogliere tre milioni di visitatori all'anno e migliaia di berlinesi ogni giorno, e di offrire cinquecento nuovi posti di lavoro.

Attraverso tre portali sempre aperti e due corti pubblicamente accessibili, le piazze circostanti si saldano con i cortili interni del nuovo Berliner Schloss - Humboldt Forum in un unico spazio pubblico, che si può definire la *Piazza Grande* del Centro di Berlino.

The Great Piazza of the Centre of Berlin

By virtue of five portal-city gates and three courtyard-squares, the new Berlin Palace could be described as a *city in the form of a palace*, capable of welcoming three million visitors a year and thousands of Berliners every day, and offering five hundred new jobs.

Through three always open portals and two public accessible courtyards, the surrounding squares merge with the inner courtyards of the new Berliner Schloss - Humboldt Forum into one unique public space, which could be defined the *Great Piazza* of the Centre of Berlin.

Anmerkungen	Note	Notes
1 Bundestagsbeschluss vom 4. Juli 2002, Drucksache 14/9660, in: *Auslobungstext. Internationaler Realisierungswettbewerb »Wiedererrichtung des Berliner Schlosses. Bau des Humboldt-Forums im Schlossareal Berlin«*, Bundesministerium für Verkehr, Bau und Stadtentwicklung, 2008, S. 89 f. (S. 90)	1 Risoluzione del Bundestag del 4 luglio 2002, Drucksache 14/9660, in: *Auslobungstext. Internationaler Realisierungswettbewerb «Wiedererrichtung des Berliner Schlosses. Bau des Humboldt-Forums im Schlossareal Berlin»*, Ministero del Traffico, dell'Edilizia e dello Sviluppo urbano, 2008, p. 89 f. (p. 90)	1 BT-Decision of 4 July 2002, document 14/9660, quoted from: Auslobungstext. Internationaler Realisierungswettbewerb "*Wiedererrichtung des Berliner Schlosses. Bau des Humboldt-Forums im Schlossareal Berlin*", Federal Ministry of Traffic, Building and Urban Development, 2008, p. 89 f. (p. 90)
2 Vgl.: Uta Hassler und Winfried Nerdinger (Hg.), *Das Prinzip Rekonstruktion*, Zürich 2010; Winfried Nerdinger mit Markus Eisen und Hilde Strobl (Hg.), *Geschichte der Rekonstruktion – Konstruktion der Geschichte*, München 2010	2. cf.: Uta Hassler und Winfried Nerdinger (a cura di), *Das Prinzip Rekonstruktion*, Zürich 2010; Winfried Nerdinger mit Markus Eisen und Hilde Strobl (a cura di), *Geschichte der Rekonstruktion – Konstruktion der Geschichte*, München 2010	2 see: Uta Hassler und Winfried Nerdinger (Eds.), *Das Prinzip Rekonstruktion*, Zürich 2010; Winfried Nerdinger mit Markus Eisen und Hilde Strobl (Eds.), *Geschichte der Rekonstruktion – Konstruktion der Geschichte*, München 2010
3 Plutarco, *Vite parallele, Teseo e Romolo*, hrsg. von Barbara Scardigli, Milano 2003, S. 187	3 Plutarco, *Vite parallele, Teseo e Romolo*, a cura di Barbara Scardigli, Milano 2003, p. 187	3 Plutarch, *Parallel Lives, Theseus and Romulus*, edited by Barbara Scardigli, Milano 2003, p. 187
4 Leon Battista Alberti, *De re aedificatoria*, Milano 1966, Band I, S. 520	4 Leon Battista Alberti, *De re aedificatoria*, Milano 1966, tomo I, p. 520	4 Leon Battista Alberti, *De re aedificatoria*, Milano 1966, volume I, p. 520
5 Karl Friedrich Schinkel, *Schinkel's Gutachten über die Erhaltung der Statuen auf dem Königlichen Schlosse zu Berlin*, in: *Aus Schinkel's Nachlaß. Reisetagebücher, Briefe und Aphorismen. Mitgetheilt und mit einem Verzeichniß sämmtlicherWerke Schinkel's* versehen von Alfred Freiherr von Wolzogen. Dritter Band, Berlin 1863, S. 163, 164	5 Karl Friedrich Schinkel, *Schinkel's Gutachten über die Erhaltung der Statuen auf dem Königlichen Schlosse zu Berlin*, in: *Aus Schinkel's Nachlaß. Reisetagebücher, Briefe und Aphorismen. Mitgetheilt und mit einem Verzeichniß sämmtlicher Werke Schinkel's*, corredato da Alfred Freiherr von Wolzogen. tomo III, Berlin 1863, pp. 163, 164	5 Karl Friedrich Schinkel, *Schinkel's Gutachten über die Erhaltung der Statuen auf dem Königlichen Schlosse zu Berlin*, in: *Aus Schinkel's Nachlaß. Reisetagebücher, Briefe und Aphorismen. Mitgetheilt und mit einem Verzeichniß sämmtlicher Werke Schinkel's*, illustrated by Alfred Freiherr von Wolzogen, volume III, Berlin 1863, pp. 163, 164
6 Adolf Loos, *Sämtliche Schriften*, Wien, München 1962, Band I, S. 318	6 Adolf Loos, *Sämtliche Schriften*, Wien, München 1962, tomo I, p. 318	6 Adolf Loos, *Sämtliche Schriften*, Wien, München 1962, volume I, p. 318
7 Leon Battista Alberti, *De re aedificatoria* (wie Anmerkung 4), S. 782	7 Leon Battista Alberti, *De re aedificatoria* (vedi nota 4), p. 782	7 Leon Battista Alberti, *De re aedificatoria* (see note 4), p. 782
8 Johann Wolfgang von Goethe, *Italienische Reise*, Goethes Werke, Band 11. *Autobiographische Schriften*. Dritter Band, München 1978, S. 52f.	8 Johann Wolfgang von Goethe, *Italienische Reise*, Goethes Werke, Band 11. *Autobiographische Schriften*. Dritter Band, München 1978, p. 52 e seguenti	8 Johann Wolfgang von Goethe, *Italienische Reise, Goethes Werke*, Band 11. *Autobiographische Schriften*. Dritter Band, München 1978, p. 52 and following

Anhang   **Appendice**   **Appendix**

Verzeichnis der Projektbeteiligten

Bauherr
Bundesrepublik Deutschland, vertreten durch die »Stiftung Humboldt Forum im Berliner Schloss«

Architekturentwurf
Prof. Franco Stella, Vicenza

Planung und Realisation
Franco Stella Berliner Schloss – Humboldt Forum PG (Projektgemeinschaft zwischen: Franco Stella, Architetto; Hilmer & Sattler und Albrecht, Gesellschaft von Architekten mbH; Detlef Krugs Baumanagement Berlin GmbH)

Projektleiter
Herman Duquesnoy, Sigurd Hauer, Peter Westermann, Michelangelo Zucchini, Fabian Hegholz (Skulpturenrekonstruktion)

Baumanagementleiter
Detlef Krug mit Alexander Scholz und Uwe Otte

Vorstudien für die Rekonstruktion der Barockfassaden
Stuhlemmer Architekten

Ausstellungsgestaltung
RAM, Ralph Appelbaum Associates

Corporate Design
Holzer Kobler Architekturen

Gebäudeleitsystem
Gourdin & Müller

Fachprojekte
— Tragwerksplanung: ARGE TPW (Wetzel & von Seht, Krone und Pichler Ingenieure)
— Technische Gebäude-Ausrüstung: ILA - Inros Lackner (Heizung, Lüftung, Sanitär von 2009 bis 2012); Winter (Heizung, Lüftung, Sanitär von 2012 bis 2016); HTES (Heizung und Lüftung ab 2016); ILA- Inros Lackner (Lüftung von 2016 bis 2019); Karoplan (Sanitär und Sprinklerung ab 2016); IGEA (Sanitär, Entwässerung Außenbereich); Geothermie Neubrandenburg (Gebäudekühlung ab 2016); Arge Innius DÖ-Innius GTD (Elektroplanung); OPB - Obermeyer (Schwachstrom und Gebäudeautomation bis 2019); ISA Saupe (OÜ Schwachstrom ab 2017); Eurolabors (Laborplanung ab

Lista dei partecipanti al progetto

Committente
Repubblica Federale Tedesca, rappresentata dalla «Stiftung Humboldt Forum im Berliner Schloss»

Progetto di architettura
Prof. Franco Stella, Vicenza

Progettazione e direzione lavori
Franco Stella Berliner Schloss – Humboldt Forum PG (Gruppo di progettazione tra: Franco Stella, Architetto; Hilmer & Sattler und Albrecht, Gesellschaft von Architekten mbH; Detlef Krugs Baumanagement Berlin GmbH)

Direttori progettazione
Herman Duquesnoy, Sigurd Hauer, Peter Westermann, Michelangelo Zucchini, Fabian Hegholz (ricostruzione di sculture)

Responsabili direzione lavori
Detlef Krug con Alexander Scholz e Uwe Otte

Studi preliminary per la ricostruzione delle facciate barocche
Stuhlemmer Architekten

Progetto allestimenti espositivi
RAM, Ralph Appelbaum Associates

Corporate Design
Holzer Kobler Architekturen

Segnaletica
Gourdin & Müller

Progetti specialistici
— Progettazione strutturale: ARGE TPW (Wetzel & Ingegneri von Seht, Krone e Pichler)
— Attrezzature tecniche per l'edilizia: ILA – Inros Lackner (riscaldamento, ventilazione, sanificazione dal 2009 al 2012); Inverno (riscaldamento, ventilazione, idraulica dal 2012 al 2016); HTES (riscaldamento e ventilazione dal 2016); ILA - Inros Lackner (ventilazione dal 2016 al 2019); Karoplan (impianto idraulico e impianto sprinkler dal 2016); IGEA (impianto sanitario, drenaggio esterno); Geotermia Neubrandenburg (raffreddamento dell'edificio da 2016); Arge Innius DÖ-Innius GTD (pianificazione elettrica); OPB - Obermeyer (corrente a bassa tensione) e auto-

List of project participants

Client
Federal Republic of Germany, represented by the "Stiftung Humboldt Forum im Berliner Schloss"

Architectural design
Prof. Franco Stella, Vicenza

Planning and realisation
Franco Stella Berliner Schloss – Humboldt Forum PG (Project group between: Franco Stella, Architetto; Hilmer & Sattler und Albrecht, Gesellschaft von Architekten mbH; Detlef Krugs Baumanagement Berlin GmbH)

Project leaders
Herman Duquesnoy, Sigurd Hauer, Peter Westermann, Michelangelo Zucchini, Fabian Hegholz (reconstruction of sculptures)

Construction manager
Detlef Krug with Alexander Scholz and Uwe Otte

Preliminary studies for the reconstruction of the Baroque façades
Stuhlemmer Architekten

Exhibition design
RAM, Ralph Appelbaum Associates

Corporate Design
Holzer Kobler Architekturen

Building guidance system
Gourdin & Müller

Specialist projects
— Structural design: ARGE TPW (Wetzel & von Seht, Krone and Pichler Engineers)
— Technical building equipment: ILA - Inros Lackner (heating, ventilation, sanitation from 2009 to 2012); Winter (heating, ventilation, plumbing from 2012 to 2016); HTES (heating and ventilation from 2016); ILA - Inros Lackner (ventilation from 2016 to 2019); Karoplan (plumbing and sprinkler system from 2016); IGEA (sanitary, drainage exterior); Geothermie Neubrandenburg (building cooling from 2016); Arge Innius DÖ-Innius GTD (electrical planning); OPB - Obermeyer (low voltage current and building automation until 2019); ISA Saupe (OÜ weak current from 2017); Eurolabors (laboratory planning from 2015); IBS (kitchen planning from

Anhang

2015); IBS (Küchenplanung ab 2015); itv Ingenieurgesellschaft (Theater-Veranstaltungs- und Sicherheitstechnik, ab 2016); BBM (Medientechnik ab 2020)
— Brandschutzplanung: BPK Brandschutzplanung
— Baulogistik: RPM-REICHEL
— Bauphysik: Müller-BBM
— Geothermieplanung: Geothermie Neubrandenburg
— Lichtplanung: Lichtvision Design & Engineering

Außenanlagen Schloss-Umfeld
(im Auftrag Land Berlin): bbz Landschaftsarchitekten

Copyright Abbildungen
— Stiftung Humboldt Forum im Berliner Schloss (Zeichnungen: S. 86, 87, 88, 89, 114, 126)
— Franco Stella (Zeichnungen: S. 70, 72, 74, 76, 84/85; Fotos: S. 32, 134)
— Stefan Müller (Fotos des gebauten Schlosses)
— FS-HUF-PG (Fotos des Schlosses im Bau);
— euroluftbild de/Robert Gran (Luftfoto S. 82)

Projektdaten

Wettbewerbsentwurf (1. Preis)
2008 (Mitarbeiter: Michelangelo Zucchini)

Bauzeit
2012 – 2020

Gebäudevolumen
490.000 m³

Bruttogeschossfläche
(ober- und unterirdisch)
100.000 m²

Nutzfläche
42.000 m²

Baukosten total
677.000.000 Euro (davon 105 Millionen aus privaten Spenden)

Appendice

mazione degli edifici fino al 2019); ISA Saupe (OÜ debole corrente dal 2017); Eurolabors (pianificazione del laboratorio a partire dal 2015); IBS (pianificazione della cucina dal 2015); itv Ingenieurgesellschaft (teatro ed eventi tecnologia per eventi e sicurezza, dal 2016); BBM (tecnologia multimediale dal 2020)
— Pianificazione della protezione antincendio: BPK Brandschutzplanung
— Logistica di costruzione: RPM-REICHEL
— Fisica dell'edificio: Müller-BBM
— Pianificazione geotermica: Geothermie Neubrandenburg
— Progetto illuminotecnico: Lichtvision Design & Engineering

Sistemazione aree esterne (su incarico del Senato di Berlino): bbz Landschaftsarchitekten

Copyright Immagini
— Stiftung Humboldt Forum im Berliner Schloss (disegni: pp. 86, 87, 88, 89, 114, 126)
— Franco Stella (disegni: pp. 70, 72, 74, 76, 84/85; foto: pp. 32, 134)
— Stefan Müller (foto del Castello costruito)
— FS-HUF-PG (foto del Castello in costruzione)
— euroluftbild de/Robert Gran (foto aerea p. 82)

Dati di progetto

Progetto di concorso (1° premio)
2008 (collaboratore: Michelangelo Zucchini)

Tempo della costruzione
2012 – 2020

Volume dell'edificio
490.000 m³

Superfice lorda
(fuori e dentro terra)
100.000 m²

Superfice utile
42.000 m²

Costo totale
677.000.000 Euro
(di cui 105 milioni da donazioni private)

Appendix

2015); itv Ingenieurgesellschaft (theatre and event event and security technology, from 2016); BBM (media technology from 2020)
— Fire protection planning: BPK Brandschutzplanung
— Construction logistics: RPM-REICHEL
— Building physics: Müller-BBM
— Geothermal planning: Geothermie Neubrandenburg
— Lighting design: Lichtvision Design & Engineering

Landscaping project for the exterior areas
(commissioned by the Berlin Senate): bbz Landschaftsarchitekten

Copyright images
— Stiftung Humboldt Forum im Berliner Schloss (drawings: p. 86, 87, 88, 89, 114, 126)
— Franco Stella (drawings: p. 70, 72, 74, 76, 84/85; photos: p. 32, 134)
— Stefan Müller (photos of the constructed Berlin Palace)
— FS-HUF-PG (photos of the Berlin Palace under construction)
— euroluftbild de/Robert Gran (aerial photo p. 82)

Project data

Competition design (1st prize)
2008 (collaboratore: Michelangelo Zucchini)

Construction period
2012 – 2020

Building volume
490.000 m³

Gross floor area
(above and below ground)
100.000 m²

Usable area
42.000 m²

Total construction costs
677.000.000 Euro (of which 105 millions from private donations)

Impressum

Sofern Bezeichnungen in männlicher Form verwendet werden, handelt es sich um ein generisches Maskulinum. Damit sind stets und selbstverständlich sowohl weibliche als auch männliche oder diverse Personen gemeint.

Lektorat: Diethelm Kaiser

Gestaltung: sans serif
Umschlagfoto: Stefan Müller

Druck + Bindung: Graspo, Zlin

Bibliografische Angaben der Deutschen Nationalbibliothek: Die Deutsche Nationalbibliothek verzeichnet diese Publikation in der Deutschen Nationalbibliografie; detaillierte bibliografische Angaben sind im Internet über https://www.dnb.de abrufbar.

Wasmuth & Zohlen Verlag Berlin
Potsdamer Str. 98a
10785 Berlin
www.wasmuth-verlag.de

© 2022 Wasmuth & Zohlen Verlag, Berlin
und die Autoren

Alle Rechte vorbehalten

ISBN 978 3 8030 2383 4

Colophon

Lettore: Diethelm Kaiser

Design: sans serif
Foto in copertina: Stefan Müller

Stampa + legatoria: Graspo, Zlin

Dati bibliografici della Deutsche Nationalbibliothek: la biblioteca nazionale tedesca elenca questa pubblicazione nella bibliografia nazionale tedesca; informazioni bibliografiche dettagliate sono disponibili sul sito https://www.dnb.de.

Wasmuth & Zohlen Verlag Berlin
Potsdamer Str. 98a
10785 Berlin
www.wasmuth-verlag.de

© 2022 Wasmuth & Zohlen Verlag, Berlin
e gli autori

Tutti i diritti riservati

Imprint

Lector: Diethelm Kaiser

Design: sans serif
Cover photo: Stefan Müller

Print + bindery: Graspo, Zlin

Bibliographic data of the German Nationalbibliothek: The Deutsche Nationalbibliothek lists this publication in the German National Bibliography; detailed bibliographic information is available on the internet at https://www.dnb.de.

Wasmuth & Zohlen Verlag Berlin
Potsdamer Str. 98a
10785 Berlin
www.wasmuth-verlag.de

© 2022 Wasmuth & Zohlen Verlag, Berlin
and the authors

All rights reserved